GOD, HELP ME

God,
Help Me

How to **GROW**

in Prayer

JIM BECKMAN

SERVANT
BOOKS

PUBLISHED BY ST. ANTHONY MESSENGER PRESS
CINCINNATI, OHIO

Excerpts from *Theology and Sanity*, by Frank Sheed, ©1978, used by permission of Ignatius Press. Excerpts from *Introduction to the Devout Life*, by Francis de Sales and translated by John K. Ryan, ©1989, used by permission of The Society for the Propagation of the Faith.

Unless otherwise noted, Scripture passages have been taken from the *Revised Standard Version*, Catholic edition. Copyright 1946, 1952, 1971 by the Division of Christian Education of the National Council of Churches of Christ in the USA. Used by permission. All rights reserved.

Note: The editors of this volume have made minor changes in capitalization to some of the Scripture quotations herein. Please consult the original source for proper capitalization.

Excerpts from the English translation of the *Catechism of the Catholic Church* for the United States of America, copyright ©1994 Libreria Editrice Vaticana—United States Catholic Conference, Inc. Used with permission. Excerpts from the English translation of the *Catechism of the Catholic Church: Modifications From the* Editio Typica, copyright ©1994 Libreria Editrice Vaticana—United States Catholic Conference, Inc.

Quotations from Vatican II documents are from the Vatican Web site, www.vatican.va.

Cover design by LUCAS Art & Design, Grandville, Michigan
Book design by Jennifer Tibbits

LIBRARY OF CONGRESS CATALOGING-IN-PUBLICATION DATA

Beckman, Jim.
  God, help me : how to grow in prayer / Jim Beckman.
      p. cm.
  ISBN 978-0-86716-890-7 (pbk. : alk. paper) 1. Prayer—Catholic Church. I. Title.
  BV215.B39 2009
  248.3'2—dc22

                            2009001546

ISBN 978-0-86716-890-7

Published by Servant Books, an imprint of St. Anthony Messenger Press
28 W. Liberty St.
Cincinnati, OH 45202
www.ServantBooks.org

Printed in the United States of America.
Printed on acid-free paper.

09 10 11 12 13 5 4 3 2 1

CONTENTS

ACKNOWLEDGMENTS

I drew much of the material in this book from the formation I have received from my spiritual director, Father Scott Traynor. His formation in turn came from the Institute for Priestly Formation (IPF), a public association of the faithful dedicated to assisting in the spiritual formation of diocesan seminarians and priests. The institute is affiliated with Creighton University in Omaha, Nebraska.

Inspired by the biblical-evangelical spirituality of Ignatius of Loyola, the institute's programs present a spirituality that can inspire, motivate and thus sustain the busy daily lives of contemporary diocesan priests. This unique approach to spiritual formation has yielded a number of personal and spiritual insights for me in the context of ongoing spiritual direction. Many of the terms, operating definitions, insights and so on have become a part of my personal spirituality.

So that credit may be given where it is due, let me state here that I refer to a good deal of IPF terminology in this book. These terms are the property of the institute, and I have used them with express permission:

- ▸▸ Christian anthropology of the heart, including all references to the three levels of the heart, the surface level, the fundamentally psychological level and the deepest level or fundamentally or specifically spiritual level.
- ▸▸ The essential dynamics of prayer, including all references to acknowledge, relate, receive, respond and "schools of prayer" in the Scriptures.
- ▸▸ The treatments of wounds, including all references to wounds in the heart, managing pain and fear, and the master affects of fear and gratitude.

▸▸ The "two ways of living," including all references to fix it, figure it out, revealing, healing and unconditional love.

▸▸ The "measure of prayer," including all references to measures, honesty and consistency.

▸▸ The operating definition of Christian imagination, including all references to Christian imagination and making spiritual realities accessible and meaningful.

▸▸ The terminology and treatment of spiritual movements, including all references to consolation and desolation as drawn from Ignatian spirituality but articulated with the unique clarity and understanding of the IPF approach to spiritual formation.

▸▸ The treatment of affective movements, including all references to affective movements, thoughts, feelings and desires—especially those that are fundamentally or specifically spiritual.

And special thanks to Father Scott Traynor for his loving care and direction of both Meg and me. The gift of God through you has been renewed prayer and a renewed relationship with each other.

another book on prayer?

Before we even start, we have to address one big question: Is there really anything else to say about prayer? There are so many books already written on the topic.

Let me assure you that there *is* something to be said: maybe not new material but a rearrangement of what is already there, drawing out a unique aspect of the message for our times and specifically for young adults today. I believe that our very future depends on young adults being able to access the age-old wisdom of the Church and the saints on the topic of prayer. *You* are leading the Church into a new era. How will you be able to lead if you aren't connected in prayer to the Master? How will he guide you? How will he inspire you?

This is why I believe this book is important. Prayer is the source of *all* in our life of faith. It provides the experience of deep intimacy that our human hearts crave. Through prayer, and only through prayer, we come to a full understanding of *who* we are and *why* we are here. The answers to these very important questions are what lead to true happiness, which is what we are all searching for in the first place.

One of the great misfortunes of youth and young adult ministry in the past couple of decades has been our inability to teach people how to pray. We've perfected events and programs, but helping a young person sustain a personal and relational life of prayer is by and large something on which we have not focused enough. That fundamental poverty has left a generation defenseless against today's attacks on the faith.

Many studies in the past several years have pointed to the effects that the postmodern era has had on this generation. There is evidence that many young people today are not very rooted in their faith, yet they are more "spiritual" than ever before; they waver on traditional issues of morality, yet they intensely desire fairness and justice. And here I see a ray of hope.

No matter what the cultural influences are, you are still human. And as a human being, created in the image and likeness of God, the very life and presence of God is written on your heart (see Deuteronomy 30:6; Jeremiah 24:7; 31:33). "God himself will graciously bring about the necessary change in his people's inner nature so that their past failure to obey his laws will be replaced by both the will and the ability to do so."[1]

Whether you realize it or acknowledge it, there is something deep inside you longing to be reconnected with the very source of life that gave rise to your existence in the first place. It's in you; you can't silence it. You can gravitate toward all kinds of other things to quench this deep desire, but only God himself will satisfy you. You were made to be in a living, loving relationship with your Maker, and *nothing* else will satisfy that deep longing within you. Saint Augustine referred to this as the "restlessness" in our hearts: "Our heart is restless until it rests in you."[2] It doesn't matter what generation you come from, that is a reality of *all* humanity.

Though that reality exists, we must also acknowledge the uniqueness of our times. This generation has had a number of influencing factors that have shaped the way that it looks at the world and the people in it. I believe that these factors have had an even more dramatic impact on prayer. The unique worldview that a postmodern culture fosters is one that diminishes our ability to connect with God in prayer.

Because of these factors there is a need to "relearn" prayer in our times. How do we navigate all the cultural influences? How do we tap into the deep human realities within us, realities that transcend time and culture, and allow these realities to drive us into a deeper life of prayer? How do we achieve intimacy with God in prayer when everything in our culture is driving us away from intimacy?

If questions like these pique your interest, if you desire to connect intimately with God in prayer, then read on. The wisdom that answers these questions has always been here, deep in the tradition and writings of our Church. I hope to unpack it and make it accessible to our times and specifically to your generation in a new way.

prayer for our times:
real and authentic

why prayer is important

I was sitting across from my spiritual director, on probably my third or fourth visit with him. Several months earlier I had had a "first meet" to discuss whether or not I would be a good fit as his directee. I remembered saying to him that I was looking for a spiritual director who could help me really "go there," someone who could help me navigate spiritual depths. That's what a good spiritual director does: help you grow in a life of prayer. Yet here I was now, months later, heading in for another session and not experiencing much depth.

We prayed, and then my director asked his typical, "So what's up?"

I responded, "Well, it's been really busy lately…"

He abruptly interrupted me. "Stop! The next thing you're going to say is something like, 'and I really haven't been praying as regularly as I should.'"

There was an awkward silence. He had taken the words right out of my mouth. He let the silence hang there for a bit and then said, "That's what you've said for the past four months, every time we've gotten together."

Another awkward silence. I really didn't know what to say.

My spiritual director finally asked, "So what's it going to take, Jim?"

I looked at him quizzically, not sure what he meant.

"What's it going to take to convince you?"

Again, a questioning look. I was genuinely confused.

"What's it going to take to convince you that there's nothing more important that you can do every day than spend time in prayer?"

Wow, there I sat. Not even five minutes into the session, and I was knocked out! I had thoughts running through my head like a firestorm. Every time I would think of something to say, I would realize how stupid it was—just a lame excuse. And my spiritual director didn't rescue me. In fact, several times during my mental gymnastics, I looked up at him only to get a questioning look, which for some reason really annoyed me. He had nailed me, and I knew it.

This torture seemed to go on forever. The more I wrestled with his question, the more I realized that there just wasn't an adequate answer. Then it hit me: I really *wasn't* convinced that prayer was important. I mean, if I was convinced, prayer would happen, right? I would find time, no matter how busy I was. I would *make* time.

Something huge happened to me that day. I admitted to myself that I didn't really believe that I needed God. I thought that I could serve him and live for him without spending intimate time with him. It sounds terrible when you say it out loud, but that was the way I was living. I let the words ring in my own mind: I actually believed that I didn't *need* to pray! I wept.

I don't know how long I cried. I was completely unaware of my spiritual director. With my admission came a flood of other realizations: How could I be a spiritual leader for others if I wasn't praying? How could God do the healing works in me I knew he wanted to do if I didn't spend time with him? And *why* wasn't I convinced that prayer was important? How could I be in love with someone I hardly spent any time with? My lack of prayer seemed like clear evidence that I wasn't really in love with God.

> I don't think there is anyone who needs God's help and grace as much as I do. Sometimes I feel so help-less and weak. I think that is why God uses me.
>
> —Mother Teresa[1]

RETURNING TO MY FIRST LOVE

It hadn't always been like that. Back in college there were times when I would pray for hours at a time. I enjoyed being with God, reading the Bible and singing worship songs. There was a newness back then to this relationship, sort of a honeymoon time.

But as time went on, prayer became more functional. It was something I knew I needed to do. I wonder whether the motivation was that I thought people expected me to pray or that I really wanted to spend time with God.

Don't get me wrong: I had many experiences of the power of prayer; I even had many deep encounters with the Lord. But my prayer wasn't consistent. I would encounter God in worship at conferences, on retreats and sometimes even in my personal prayer. But there was something missing.

That day with my spiritual director was the beginning of a shift in my life. It marked a return to a love that over time I had allowed to grow distant, even cold. I decided that nothing was more important than prayer. There have been days since when lunchtime has been my prayer time. I have cancelled "important" meetings so I could take time to pray.

It's not always easy to find that time, especially on days when I'm running from the moment I wake up until the moment I lay my head down at night. (That's what working several jobs, being married and having five children can do with your time.) But even on those days I have this deep conviction that I can't make it without stopping to breathe with God.

I previously approached prayer as a kind of drug. I used it to help me feel close to God, to give me experiences of his presence. But as with a drug, I could choose when to take it, and I could sometimes go without it.

Prayer now has become more like air. It's not really an option: I can't breathe without it; I can't live without it.

Prayer is a relationship with the Lord of all. I've become convinced that there's nothing more important I can do in my day than take some time to be with my Lord. I *need* him, and I know that now in a way I didn't before.

> Those who do not pray habitually, no matter how faith-filled or pious, will not achieve full spiritual maturity. They will not acquire peace of soul because they will always experience excessive disquietude and view things according to their human or worldly significance. Thus, they will always suffer from vanity, selfishness, self-centeredness, ambition, meanness of heart, judgment, and an unhealthy willfulness and attachment to their opinions. Those who do not pray may acquire human wisdom and prudence, but not true spiritual freedom or a deep and radical purification of heart. They will not be able to grasp the depths of divine mercy or know how to make it known to others. Their judgments will always end up short-sighted, mistaken, and contemptible. They will never be able to walk God's ways, which are far different from what many—even those who have committed themselves to a life in the spirit—imagine them to be.
>
> —Jacques Philippe[2]

IDENTITY AND MISSION

As I have grown in my experience of prayer, I have come to experience the fact that prayer is meant to draw us into intimacy with God—Father, Son and Holy Spirit. Experiences of this Trinitarian intimacy have a way of helping me understand who I am. And by its very nature, that is what prayer does: It informs and inspires my core identity.

In *Gaudium et Spes*, one of the Vatican II documents, there's a great line that John Paul II liked to quote: "Christ, the final Adam, by the revelation of the mystery of the Father and his love, fully reveals man to man himself and makes his supreme calling clear" (*Gaudium et Spes*, 22). In other words, Jesus became man to reveal God to man and to reveal *man* to *himself*. Spending time with Jesus can only help me come to a greater understanding of myself. My very identity is informed and inspired whenever I spend time with him.

And guess what, when I come to a deeper understanding of who I am, that has a tendency to give me a greater sense of why I'm here. What's my purpose in life? Why did God put me here? It all gets greater clarity through the movements of prayer, for it is Jesus who "makes his supreme calling clear."

"Why am I here? What's my life all about anyway?" I hear questions like these all the time. There are whole sections in book-stores devoted to the topic.

It's so simple really. Who better to help you understand why you're here than the one who made you? It is his deepest desire to be in a loving relationship with you and, through that relationship, to inform and inspire who you are and what you do in this life that he has given you.

Prayer is the access point to this kind of clarity. If you want to know who you are and why you're here, start praying every day.

> In the silence of the heart God speaks. If you face God in prayer and silence, God will speak to you. Then you will know that you are nothing. It is only when you realize your nothingness, your emptiness, that God can fill you with Himself. Souls of prayer are souls of great silence.

> —Mother Teresa[3]

STORY AND RELATIONSHIP

Prayer is not just about us; it's not just about the experiences we desire to have with God. Prayer is about *our* part in the big story of salvation. When we see ourselves as a part of this larger story, we feel connected, rooted in something bigger than ourselves. This perspective gives us meaning and purpose beyond our own lives.

> People who grow up without a sense of how yesterday has affected today are unlikely to have a strong sense of how today affects tomorrow. They are unlikely to understand in a bone-deep way how the decisions they make now will shape and affect their future.
>
> —William K. Kilpatrick[4]

Our prayer is not a series of random attempts to reach God but rather a journey that we're on. Seeing this larger picture, seeing ourselves connected to the larger story, gives prayer a context. Indeed, prayer is one of the primary ways we play our part in God's plan of salvation.

I see an analogy to my relationships with my family. My wife, my kids: Many things happen with them in a given week that I can't predict. If I am not in daily communication with each one of them, in relationship, chances are I won't recognize something happening. And depending on how distant I am from the person affected, he or she may not even tell me about it. I would miss it.

Yet there are many days when spending time with my family is not very fulfilling emotionally: I am just with them, and they are with me. But it is exactly this type of time that sets us up for the bigger, more significant experiences—those moments that make memories and cement our relationships even more.

Because prayer is all about a relationship with the Trinity, the same principle holds true. If you're not spending regular, consistent time in prayer, you may miss some or even all of the deep connecting moments with the Lord that will cement your relationship with him. Even when you try to pray and God doesn't seem to show up, don't stop praying; rather you should see this situation as his helping you develop perseverance. You will also find a deeper appreciation of the times when God sets you on fire. In fact, persevering through times of desolation bears fruit in your relationship over the long haul. Countless saints will testify to this.

The other thing that helps me pray is the realization that there is very little in prayer that depends on me. I can't make myself have deep spiritual experiences. I can't create consolation for myself. I can't make up a word from God or make myself any holier. All of that depends on God. His movements are his, and I can't do anything to make them happen.

The only things that I bring to the mix are consistently showing up for prayer and the disposition of my heart when I am there. With so little to contribute, I have decided that I want to make sure I'm doing my part every day.

WHAT'S YOUR EXCUSE?

As you read this, what thoughts are running through your head? If you were sitting with a spiritual director and being asked what it was going to take to convince you to pray, what arguments would you give? These arguments form in all of our minds, so let's take a few minutes to deal with them.

No Time

Probably the most common reason for not praying is that I'm too busy: There's just not enough time. That's the excuse that came to my mind, four months in a row! You don't have to go down this path very far to realize how lame an excuse it is.

Again, put prayer in the context of any relationship in your life. What kind of relationships would you have with people if you never spent any time with them?

The way we spend our time tends to reveal what we place value on. One author I read on this topic observed with amusement that no one ever died of hunger because of not having time to eat. There are things we do with our time every day, and if we track our activity, we'll see what is truly important to us. If prayer is something we place value on, we'll make time for it.

My encouragement is to shift your perspective to one based on relationship. When we see prayer in this context, it's hard to justify having no time for it. If God is one of the people with whom you have a relationship, how much time will you spend with him? Do you relate to him first? If not, why not? He is inviting you into a deeper relationship of love with him and inviting you to make your relationship with him the highest priority in your life.

My "Ministry"

Some people may be tempted to think that they can't pray because they are so busy doing good things: They have ministry plans or time that needs to be spent with family. We could address this as we did the above argument about time in general, but this has a unique dimension.

It is easy to think that our charitable works are more important than prayer. But this is a temptation directly from the enemy! (We're going to talk more about the enemy in chapter four. For now it's crucial to understand that there *is* an enemy who is ruthlessly devoted to *your* demise. Saint Ignatius calls him the "enemy of human nature." He says that "there is no beast so fierce on the face of the earth as the enemy of human nature in following out his damnable intention with such growing malice."[5])

Look to John 15: "I am the vine, you are the branches. He who abides in me, and I in him, he it is that bears much fruit, for apart from me you can do nothing" (verse 5).

Hear that? Jesus didn't say that we can't do much without him; he said we can do *nothing*. It is a complete fallacy to think that we can do any good thing apart from God. In fact, it is only when we are tapped into him through a life of prayer, even when the prayer is dry and arid, that we experience any tangible fruit in our efforts.

There are many quotes I could put here—from John Paul II, Mother Teresa and countless saints. They *all* came to the same conviction and in their own lives started praying *more* in times of great busyness. Saint John of the Cross captures it the best, I think:

> Let those who go bustling about, who think they can transform the world with their exterior works and preaching, take note that they would profit the Church more and be far more pleasing to God...if they spent half as much time abiding with God in prayer.... Certainly, they would accomplish more and with less toil with one work than they would now with a thousand works thanks to their prayers and the increased spiritual strength from which they would benefit. Otherwise, their lives would be reduced to making a lot of noise and accomplishing little more than nothing, if not nothing at all, or indeed at times even doing harm.[6]

The scary part for me as I read this is "even doing harm": working hard, spending myself in ministry efforts and serving others, only to find out that all along I was actually harming people because of my stubborn resistance to a life of prayer. I can't do any good thing without starting in prayer. I can't share Christ with others if he is not in me first. My life needs to be filled with his life, and then my ministry efforts simply become a sharing of what he has already given to me.

> [Saint Bernard said,] "If you are wise, you will be reservoirs and not channels."... The channels let the water flow away, and do not retain a drop. But the reservoir is first filled, and then, without emptying itself, pours out its overflow, which is ever renewed, over the fields which it waters.[7]

We are not meant to be channels, just moving things from here to there, even good things that we have heard or learned. We are designed to be reservoirs, filled to capacity with the very life of God, even overflowing. It is the overflow that becomes our ministry.

Constant Prayer

Another common thing I hear is the argument for what I would call casual prayer. "I pray when I'm driving," or, "I take my prayer time while I'm going through my day, as I'm working, or as I'm doing my daily tasks—sort of making everything I do a prayer." You may find some backing for this approach to prayer in the lives of some saints who prayed without ceasing, as Saint Paul advises (see Ephesians 6:18; 1 Thessalonians 5:17).

Though this approach has some merit, and even an air of holiness to it, if it is not combined with regular focused time in prayer, it's not going to work. You just cannot sustain a deep prayer life with this kind of distracted prayer. If you did a little research on those saints, you would find that they had a very full and rich personal prayer life, and the desire to make their entire day a prayer flowed from that focused time. They would have never encouraged casual prayer as the only way to pray.

Put it in the context of relationship again: What relationship in your life would survive such an approach? If my primary time of communication with my wife was while we were driving somewhere together or while I was doing my daily tasks, I probably wouldn't be married anymore. We can have some conversations like that, but for the most part, my wife looks for my full attention. Does God deserve any less from me? And if my desire is for intimate connection with him, do I deserve any less?

I Want to Be Real!

I have also heard many young people say that they don't pray regularly because their "heart is not in it." Their thought is, "I would not want to pray simply out of obligation. That would seem so fake, so unreal."

This type of thinking seems to come from a form of sincerity. Wanting to pray with your whole heart is certainly a good intention. Refusing to have anything less might seem to evidence that you are being true to yourself, enjoying freedom and spontaneity in your relationship with God. But in reality it's a false sense of sincerity.

The focus in this approach is you, not God. Ultimately that is not what prayer is all about. And you are not really free if you are enslaved to your own emotions.

Once again, this approach falls short when put in the context of a relationship. We are constantly called to love, serve and care for others we are in relationship with, even when we don't feel like it. Is that somehow insincere? If we stretch beyond our feelings and spend time with someone, even when our heart is not in it, is that fake? Actually it's more real and sincere when we love *despite* our feelings. The true measure of love is faithfulness and constancy, pushing through our feelings to love another.

I'm Not Worthy

It is common to experience thoughts and feelings of unworthiness when we have fallen or when we struggle with habitual sin. The temptation is to think that prayer is fruitless: I have done such evil things, and nothing seems to be changing. I would be better off if I stopped praying altogether.

Lies! Lies from within; lies from evil that is the enemy of our human nature! Don't believe them. Listen to these words from Saint Teresa of Avila, a doctor of the Church and one of the great writers on spirituality:

> I repeat that no one who has begun to practise prayer should be discouraged and say: "If I am going to fall again, it will be better for me not to go on practising prayer." I think it will be if such a person gives up prayer and does not amend his evil life; but, if he does not give up, he may have confidence that prayer will bring him into the haven of light. This was a matter about which the devil kept plaguing me, and I suffered so much through thinking myself lacking in humility for continuing prayer, when I was so wicked, that, as I have said, for a year and a half I gave it up—or at any rate for a year: I am not quite sure about the six months. This would have been nothing less than plunging into hell—nor was it: there was no need for any devils to send me there. Oh, God help me, how terribly blind I was! How well the devil succeeds in his purpose when he pursues us like this! The deceiver knows that if a soul perseveres in practising prayer it will be lost to him, and that, by the goodness of God, all the relapses into which he can lead it will only help it to make greater strides onward in His service. And this is a matter of some concern to the devil.[8]

This argument too could be put in the context of relationship. If you have struggled and been unfaithful toward someone you love deeply, is your response to pull away from the person? To hide your unfaithfulness and avoid dealing with it all? If you do so, it will only be a matter of time before the relationship is lost.

The same holds true with our relationship with God. When we fall short, when we have been unfaithful, that is exactly when we are in desperate need of him. Saint James advises, "Draw near to God and he will draw near to you" (James 4:8).

CONVINCED?

I'm sure other arguments may form in your mind, and I could probably go on forever dealing with them one by one. But I hope the few that we have addressed here develop the pattern to deal with all others. Every argument against regular, consistent, daily prayer simply needs to be put in the context of a loving, intimate relationship. Each and every argument loses its force in that context.

Here's the bottom line: Will you decide that prayer is the most important activity of each and every day for you? What's it going to take to convince you that this is true? If you were in my situation, sitting with your spiritual director and being challenged the way I was, how would you respond?

I look back on that day now with such gratitude. I knew even then of my spiritual director's love for me. In his challenge I felt his desire to see me experience everything he knew I was missing rather than to chastise me for my shallow prayer life. The experience has drawn me more deeply into a consistent, daily life of prayer, which over the past several years has borne tremendous fruit in my life.

You may find yourself saying, "Yes! I want to pray more. I desire a relationship with God. But why is it so hard?"

I truly believe that our times and our culture have severely handicapped us when it comes to prayer. Many factors have contributed to a diminished capacity for the intimacy in prayer that God desires us to experience. Before delving into prayer itself, I believe it is crucial for us to explore those cultural realities.

cultural realities

We might see the dynamics of our culture more clearly by looking at other cultures and a different time, completely distinct from ours. Let's go back to ancient Egypt, to the time of Moses.

I hope you're familiar with this powerful story of God's power and faithfulness. My kids love the cartoon version, *The Prince of Egypt*. You might prefer to read the original in the book of Exodus.

I want to focus on a particular part: after Moses talked with Pharaoh many times, after he performed several miracles, after all the plagues, God finally told Moses how he was going to deliver Israel from the hand of Pharaoh. He had Moses tell the people to find an unblemished lamb, kill it in public and then put its blood on their doorposts (see Exodus 12:1–8).

This command leads to some puzzling questions: Why a lamb? And why kill it? Why kill it in public? Why put its blood on the doorposts? Have you ever thought about why God asked them to do all this?

PROBLEMS WITH PAGANS

To understand the answers to these questions, we have to go back to how the Israelites ended up in Egypt in the first place and what happened to them while they were there.

At the end of Genesis, we read of the incredible drama of Joseph and his brothers: They sold him into slavery, God miraculously raised him up as a leader in Egypt, second only to Pharaoh himself, and Joseph thus saved his people from famine and death.

The book of Genesis ends with Joseph forgiving his brothers and telling them that what they meant for evil, God used for good.

God used Joseph to save his people, and the entire Israelite nation migrated to Egypt. But the book of Exodus begins with a new time and a new king in Egypt, who didn't even know Joseph. Now, wouldn't you think the story of Joseph would be told for a long time: a Hebrew who came to their land as a slave, interpreted the dreams of Pharaoh, was raised up as a leader in all of Egypt and then saved the nation from famine? How could that story not be known for centuries?

When the Bible says that the new king did not know Joseph, it means that he refused to acknowledge Joseph and his mighty works. A footnote in the *New American Bible* tells us, "This king ignored the services that Joseph had rendered to Egypt."[1] He had a new agenda, a new plan for the future. And this plan did not leave room for the Israelites.

The Egyptian culture of this time was one of many gods: the sun, the moon, the weather, the river, animals and so forth. It seems they had a god for everything. Many of the worshipping practices involved sexual immorality. There was an inordinate attraction to the body and to sex.

As the Egyptians became more and more absorbed in themselves, their false gods and their pleasures, they had little time for anything else, especially the nuisance of children, who were often by-products of the sexual immorality. The Egyptians developed many ways to prevent pregnancy and to terminate pregnancies that did occur.

You're probably wondering by now where I'm going with all this, and what does it all have to do with prayer?

Think about this: Doesn't this Egyptian culture sound a little like our culture today? A society that had no belief in the one true God and as a result fabricated many other gods; that gravitated toward all sorts of immoral behavior and was practically consumed by its own passions and lust; that became annoyed, even disdainful, toward the very fruit of its seed, its own children? The story of the Egyptian culture in the time of Moses is eerily similar to our own, and for those willing to listen, it provides lessons that we need to hear so we don't repeat history.

The Israelites were in Egypt 430 years (see Exodus 12:40), though there is some speculation among scholars about this. And during that time, generations of time, the Israelites became more and more like the Egyptians. They started taking on their practices and customs, even started worshipping their gods. After a while it was probably difficult to see much of a difference between an Israelite and an Egyptian.

We read in ensuing chapters that the Israelites begged Moses to take them back to Egypt (Exodus 16:2–3; Numbers 14:4; 20:3–5). They so longed for the comforts that they had enjoyed there that they were willing to abandon their faith in God in order to be comfortable again.

This story from the time of Moses is not new, and it won't be the last time we hear it. Unfortunately, the history repeats over and over again throughout the Old Testament. The pattern is always the same. God saves his people, and in their salvation they are strangely silent, seemingly ungrateful, almost heirs of entitlement. Over time the people grow lax in their faith and start compromising, making exceptions and rationalizing. They take on practices and customs of the people around them, instead of bringing the people around them to faith. Their behavior takes them further and further away from God and his protection.

Israel ends up being taken over by some other country, thrown into slavery or exiled. In their suffering they finally realize how stupid they were, and they cry out to God. God hears their cry and sees their suffering and, believe it or not, he's moved with compassion and reaches out to *save* them. But then the people are strangely silent, seemingly ungrateful...

You can track this pattern throughout the Old Testament. You begin to wonder, "What is wrong with these people?! Why don't they get it?!" But you don't have to reflect long to realize that this pattern is repeated over and over again in your own life.

Quick side note here: This is why the Bible is so important to us and especially to our prayer. We often can't make sense out of our own life, but when we see our life in the context of the larger story of salvation history, we can get much greater clarity. God can reveal himself to us and can reveal *us* to ourselves through the experiences of those who have gone before us. But when that "story" is lost and forgotten, we run the tragic risk of repeating their mistakes.

SOUND FAMILIAR?

I truly believe that the times we are in right now are very similar to the time of Moses. We're very much like those Israelites. We have been absorbed into the culture around us, many of us taking on its practices and customs. Some have even begun to question whether God exists. The culture has had a dramatic effect on the way we look at the world, the way we look at each other and, most importantly, the way we look at God.

If we want to "relearn" prayer in these times, it is going to take a serious dismantling of the influence that the culture has had on us. You won't be able to pray if you don't address it!

Here are some of the earmarks of our culture, the influences that are trying to steal our affections:

A godless society: Moral relativism, secular humanism and other philosophical thoughts have convinced many that God does not exist, or if he does, that he must be some type of mean, manipulative, selfish ogre. Nietzsche was one of the first to say so bluntly, "God is dead. God remains dead. And we have killed him."[2]

A popular scientist recently published a book that articulates his thoughts toward God: "The God of the Old Testament is arguably the most unpleasant character in all fiction: jealous and proud of it; a petty, unjust, unforgiving control-freak; a vindictive, bloodthirsty ethnic cleanser; a misogynistic, homophobic, racist, infanticidal, genocidal, filicidal, pestilential, megalomaniacal, sadomasochistic, capriciously malevolent bully."[3] What an incredibly misinformed interpretation of who God is!

In modern thinking, because there is seemingly no God, we should be free to do whatever we want, especially when it comes to our own bodies. Follow this thought: If there is no God, then *I* am God. And as my own god, I am free to do whatever I please.

There is a sense of spirituality in our culture, even a deep hunger for spiritual things, but it is not directed toward God. In that fundamental misdirection, society has created many "gods" in the same way the Egyptians did: money, success, technology, popularity, sex, the body, media and so on. This is nothing new in the story: "And the LORD will scatter you among the peoples, and you will be left few in number among the nations where the LORD will drive you. And there you will serve gods of wood and stone, the work of men's hands, that neither see, nor hear, nor eat, nor smell" (Deuteronomy 4:28).

An isolated society. Our modern culture has driven us away from each other. For all our technological advances, promising more connectedness and communication, we are more deprived of real intimacy than at any other time in history. "Contemporary relationships now exist within the context of technology saturated homes and lifestyles. Evidence exists to suggest that modern technology, including television, cellular phones, computers and the Internet, can be used in ways that cause and perpetuate problems in committed relationships."[4]

This culture of isolation has led many to believe that they can be completely independent, which is just not how God created us. There seems to be a resistance to community and interdependence, which are naturally human. And in this isolated society, technology seems to have become a god in itself. We are constantly trying to expand, to get newer or smaller or bigger—or just different. And technology has a way of feeding many of the other gods in the culture: isolation, independence, lust, selfishness. If I don't like what you are watching on TV, no worry, I can go to another room and watch what I want on another TV. I can have what I want, when and how I want it.

Lack of intimacy also results from a lack of love, another effect of a godless society. Many of your peers—maybe even you— have been wounded in relationships with friends and family members. Wounded people tend to not get too close to anyone because they can't risk getting hurt again.

An oversexualized society. There is a serious misunderstanding in our culture about our sexuality, a serious misunderstanding of what it means to be human. Pope Benedict XVI referred to it as an "anticulture ... expressed in a sexuality that becomes sheer irresponsible enjoyment, that makes the human person into a 'thing,' so to speak, no longer considered a person who deserves personal love which requires fidelity, but who becomes a commodity, a mere object."[5]

Many ads on TV, billboards, magazines and other media carry sexual overtones. And this is affecting people of all ages.

> Everything's happening at younger and younger ages. This phenomenon is known as "age compression." Marketers have actually employed this as a strategy to expand a product's market by pushing adult-type products, values, and attitudes on kids at younger and younger ages. What's resulted is an environment where

> what used to be for 18-year-olds is now for 6-year-olds. Today's 6-year-olds are increasingly looking, dressing, talking, and acting like yesterday's 18-year-olds. Some of the most direct effects can be seen in what children at younger and younger ages know and believe about sexuality, materialism, and violence. The children in your congregation are far less innocent and far more jaded than their peers in previous generations.[6]

The news carries stories of sexual crimes—teachers molesting students, teens and even children abusing each other. Many people find themselves addicted to Internet pornography. Such things are more than shocking; they're scary.

Pope John Paul II led a way to healing for us through his prophetic work, the *Theology of the Body*. "Man cannot live without love. He remains a being that is incomprehensible for himself, his life is senseless, if love is not revealed to him, if he does not encounter love, if he does not experience love and make it his own, if he does not participate intimately in it."[7]

A society that makes a god of youth. Today's young are glorified, and youthful traits are sought after. Many of the young want to never grow up. The youth culture, which used to be defined as thirteen to eighteen, is now defined by many as eight to thirty. Adults are often portrayed as morons, and it's the youth who save the day. They're smarter, more mature and more together than adults could ever hope to be. We have an entire generation of adults who have formed much of their outlook on life in this kind of environment, and another generation coming right behind them—*you*.

The problem is that young people are going through the most insecure, unstable time of their lives. The culture systematically removes adult influences, leaving them somewhat directionless, striving to make sense out of things on their own. Over time this has had drastic ramifications.

Fortunately, recent studies reveal that increasing percentages of young people do look to their parents and other significant adults as the primary influences in their decisions. Here's a shift in culture that we can applaud!

A lost sense of the nuclear family.

> The sexual revolution of the 1960s and 1970s combined with a changing moral climate, rising individualism and other factors to lower our collective view of marriage, thus leading to a rise in divorce....
>
> In 2004, there were 7.8 marriages per 1,000 people (2,279,000) and 3.7 divorces per 1,000 people. "The American divorce rate today is nearly twice that of 1960, but has declined slightly since hitting the highest point in our history in the early 1980s." On the surface, this may seem like a move in the right direction—and in some ways it is. But don't forget that during the same time, the number of cohabitating couples and out-of-wedlock births increased as well. Fewer and fewer people are getting married....
>
> All of these stats add up to this sad fact: The U.S. has the highest divorce rate and the highest proportion of children affected by divorce in the developed world![8]

With the divorce rate so high, there is a desire in some to change the traditional terms that refer to it: broken marriages, broken families, children wounded by divorce and so on, all seem to be negative terms that can be hurtful. However, in efforts to be sensitive to the reality of this, we have to be careful not to normalize it.

This situation was never a part of God's plan. Rather it results from the other influences of the culture—isolation, independence, sexual confusion and so on.

A culture of death. As modern culture became increasingly consumed with pleasure with seemingly little consequence, a natural move, just as with the Egyptians back in Moses' time, was to remove obstacles to that. Birth control and abortion attempt to eliminate what would prevent people from enjoying "freedom" from the consequences of their actions. There are 1.3 million abortions a year in the United States alone.[9] That's 4,000 abortions a day—an average of one baby every twenty-two seconds.

A society of "tolerance." You can find yourself in big trouble these days if you are seen as intolerant, especially in reference to someone's beliefs or lifestyle. It seems the only thing our culture is intolerant of is traditional Christian values. Before becoming pope Cardinal Joseph Ratzinger wrote:

> [T]he more relativism becomes the generally accepted way of thinking, the more it tends toward intolerance, thereby becoming a new dogmatism.... [The] relativism [of political correctness] creates the illusion that it has reached greater heights than the loftiest philosophical achievements of the past. It prescribes itself as the only way to think.... Being faithful to traditional values and to the knowledge that upholds them is labeled intolerance.... I think it is vital that we oppose this imposition of a new pseudo-enlightenment which threatens freedom of thought as well as freedom of religion.... [R]elativism [is] a kind of new "denomination" that places restrictions on religious convictions and seeks to subordinate all religions to the super-dogma of relativism.[10]

GOD'S INVITATION

My list of cultural earmarks is not meant to be comprehensive. Universities offer semester-long courses on the topic of modern culture, so we can't hope to cover it all here. My hope is to demonstrate the broad-stroke effects of the culture on our ability to approach God in prayer.

The culture fosters everything from confusion about who God is and whether or not he is even real to a deep insecurity about intimacy. These things have caused a deep rift between us and God, often without our even knowing.

I can't help but imagine that this is what it was like for the Israelites when they confronted pagan nations. They weren't planning on losing themselves in the culture around them; they weren't planning on abandoning everything they believed. But the stuff going on around them was intriguing and appealing. I'm sure theirs wasn't a headlong fall but more of a "checking it out." Over time the "testing" became something to which they gave their hearts.

We have to reflect on our own lives to see if we have fallen into the same situation. The pervasive philosophical confusion can take us down numerous paths that end in destruction. The culture will try to convince us that the truth doesn't matter.

The invitation of this book is the invitation of God through Moses: "Take...a lamb" and kill it with "the whole assembly," and then "take some of the blood, and put it on the two doorposts and the lintel of the houses" (Exodus 12:3, 6, 7). God's invitation was not only to leave Egypt, not only to find freedom from slavery to the Egyptians, but to find freedom from the slavery to one's own sin.

The lamb was one of the Egyptian gods. To kill a lamb was a capital offense, punishable by death. Notice how God asked the Israelites to kill the lamb not in the privacy of their own homes but out in the open, with "the whole assembly" present, and then to put the blood right on their doorposts for all to see. If anyone wanted to know who had killed lambs, all they had to do was look at the front doors!

God wanted the Israelites to *kill* their false gods and return to him. And he wanted that to be a public act, one that they could not turn back from, because he knew that they would be tempted to do exactly that.

One of the cumulative effects of our culture is a diminished capacity for intimacy. This results from many different influences: experiences from childhood, when trust in someone was violated; sexual wounds; isolation; lack of intimacy modeled by parents; constant busyness and lack of time for intimate connection; the constant flow of media, which saturates us and even allows us to have experiences of "false" intimacy with unreal people. This cumulative effect, I believe, has greatly impacted prayer, because prayer is all about intimacy with God—Father, Son and Holy Spirit. What greater way to destroy prayer than to wound people in such a way that they are incapable of being intimate?

There has been a strategic attack throughout all of time against our trust in God and our intimate connection with him. It was the attack against Adam and Eve, and it is the attack we experience today. If we desire to grow deeper in our experience of prayer, we must allow this wound to be healed.

This may not be a pleasant experience, for healing sometimes involves pain. The pain of healing is like the pain our moms would administer in gently cleaning our cuts and scrapes and pulling out our splinters when we were young. We trusted our moms, knowing that the pain would lead to healing. This is the pain we will experience if we allow God to love us in our brokenness. And trusting him with our wounds can lead us to a deep life of prayer.

The invitation God gave the Israelites is the same invitation he is offering us. He is inviting us on an incredible journey with him, and part of that journey is letting go of all the false idols we worship, the things we have allowed to steal our affections, and letting him love us into healing and wholeness. We can't pursue him halfway: To follow him means to let go of our sinful past.

How do we do this? It happens in prayer.

understanding prayer

straight to the heart

My six-year-old son Jonathan has a nickname in our house: "Destructo-boy!" He has this uncanny ability to break things. At times it drives me crazy, especially when he breaks something valuable, which he frequently does.

Recently I bought my wife a new cell phone. Within a week a corner of the battery cover was bent. Come to find out, it was Jonathan who did it. I was so angry! When I talked to him, though, his explanation calmed me: "Daddy, I just wanted to see what was in there!"

For a moment I saw myself in my son. I remember saying similar things to my parents. I was a curious kid, always wanting to know how things worked, wanting to take things apart. I was fascinated with engines, small motors and anything that had parts.

Once I took apart our lawn mower, piece by piece. The only problem was I couldn't remember how it all went back together.

Learning about prayer has been a lot like taking off the back of a cell phone to see what's in there or taking the mower apart to see how it works. I have come to a much deeper understanding of what all the different parts of prayer are and how they work together.

I've been praying for a long time and have had some very powerful experiences in prayer. I've experienced deep connections with God and times of incredible closeness and intimacy. Yet I was never really sure how it happened. I found myself wondering many times what I did that made it work, so that I could replicate the experience. I've read all kinds of books and even taken classes on prayer, all with a desire to go deeper. But a lack of understanding of the internal parts made that difficult.

It wasn't until a few years ago, going through spiritual direction and learning more about prayer and particularly about Ignatian spirituality, that things started really clicking for me. It's my desire in this book to share that new knowledge. I truly believe it is a collection of material that sheds new light on prayer for young adults today.

As I've said before, this knowledge has been around for a very long time: It's part of the richness we possess as Catholics. Yet many people have been unable to access it and integrate it into their lived experience of prayer.

If we "take the back off" and look at what all the parts of prayer are, we'll come up with a list that sounds a lot like the rest of the topics and chapters of this book: the human heart, spiritual movements in our heart, the enemy, the measures of prayer, the fundamental dynamics of prayer, short circuits to prayer, Christian imagination and so on. All these parts have an important role to play in our experience of prayer or our lack thereof. In fact, not being aware of these parts can actually diminish our prayer.

One of the great gifts Saint Ignatius gave us in his unique approach to spirituality is his discussion of awareness. God is laboring to love us at all times, and he is constantly at work in our lives. Ignatius encouraged becoming more aware of this activity and promptly responding to it.

Throughout the rest of this book, we are going to systematically tear prayer apart and see how it really works. We're not going to look specifically at any one type of prayer: Liturgy of the Hours, the rosary, intercessory prayer, adoration and so on. Rather we're going to look at the inner dynamics of what prayer is—*all* prayer. How do we get into a *real* and growing relationship with Jesus? How do we navigate depth in our prayer life so we're not just going through the motions, not just putting in time? It all starts with understanding where prayer takes place—in our heart.

THE HUMAN HEART

The "activity" of God that Ignatius talks about takes place primarily in our heart. So understanding our heart and how it's made up can help us become more aware of these movements.

Scripture scholar James Hastings wrote that "'[H]eart' came to signify *the seat of man's collective energies,* the focus of the personal life."[1] "The heart [is] the centre of spiritual activity."[2] The beginning of prayer requires an entry-level understanding of this "center" "of all spiritual activity."

We find references to the heart of man all through the Scriptures: it is the heart of the Israelites that God promises to "circumcise" "after their exodus from Egypt (see Deuteronomy 30:6); the prophets speak about the new, living heart that God desires to put inside us, in place of our hard and stony hearts (Ezekiel 11:19–20; 36:26–27); we're told that God will write his law upon our hearts (Jeremiah 31:33).

The Scriptures speak of the heart as the source of prayer more than a thousand times (see *CCC*, 2562). In fact, *heart* and *soul* are often used interchangeably in Scripture.[3] I hope you get the idea here: The heart is *really* important to prayer!

Check out what the *Catechism* says specifically about the heart and prayer: "The heart is the dwelling-place where I am, where I live; according to the Semitic, or Biblical expression, the heart is the place to which I withdraw. The heart is our hidden center, beyond the grasp of our reason and of others; only the Spirit of God can fathom the human heart and know it fully" (*CCC*, 2563). And in another reference: "The heart is the place of this quest and encounter" (*CCC*, 2710).

If we take a closer look at this "center" of spiritual activity, we realize that not everything that goes through our hearts can be called spiritual. How do we distinguish between things?

First, let's give a name to the stuff that moves in our hearts. You can pretty much narrow it down to thoughts, feelings and desires. These basic affective movements are the primary things that we experience moving through our hearts on any given day.

There are multiple levels to our heart where these movements happen in us.[4]

Some thoughts, feelings and desires take place just on the surface—"I'm hungry," "I'm mad," and so on. There's not a lot of depth to them, but we experience movements at that surface level hundreds of times a day.

Then there are deeper movements: thoughts, feelings and desires that begin to tap into our memories, our relationships and so on. This is what we would refer to as the "psychological level" of the heart. These deeper thoughts, feelings and desires carry a lot more weight, but they still aren't at the deepest level of the heart.

That would be the spiritual level, and it's these thoughts, feelings and desires that we really need to get in touch with, especially for prayer. They are moving at the deepest level of who we are, even though sometimes they may seem to be just on the surface.

DEEP MOVEMENTS

Thoughts, feelings and desires that move at the deepest level of our heart, the spiritual level, can be defined as *affective movements* that impact directly our relationship with God and our ability to carry out his will in our life. When Jesus was baptized in the Jordan River by John the Baptist, the Scriptures tell us that the heavens were opened, and the Spirit descended on him like a dove, and words came from the heavens saying, "This is my beloved Son, with whom I am well pleased" (Matthew 3:17). These words are right at the deepest level of Jesus' heart. Notice how they speak directly of his relationship with the Father. These words "inform" and "inspire" Jesus' very identity.

I have had experiences in prayer where God has brought me to that same passage, but the words were spoken to me, not to Jesus. This is how God can move in our hearts to inform and inspire our identity and to confirm our relationship with him.

Unfortunately though, the Holy Spirit is not the only voice at work at the deepest level of our hearts. We also hear the voices of our human spirit and of the evil spirit. The messages that God sends deep into our hearts are often mixed with messages that come from these other sources. Another hallmark of Ignatian spirituality is learning how to distinguish between the good Spirit and the enemy. We'll talk more about this in chapter four. For now though, it's absolutely critical to acknowledge that all the movements that take place on that deepest level of our heart are not necessarily from God. And those that aren't can be sources of spiritual desolation.

Our purpose here is to get in touch with those deep movements in our heart, to actually make contact with what's going on inside us. It's a struggle with prayer that we must engage. From everything we talked about in chapter two, we can see why there is a struggle: The deep poverty of our times is a diminished capacity for intimacy. Our fast-paced life, saturation with media and electronics and the wounded trust in many people combine as a formidable obstacle to what prayer fundamentally is—an intimate relationship.

Prayer requires time; it requires knowing yourself or at least a desire to know yourself better; it requires risk and honesty. Simon Tugwell wrote:

> God's word is addressed to us as we really are, not as
> we like to present ourselves; he speaks to our heart,
> not to our mask. It is not only that little bit of us

which we have, as it were, colonised and made sub-
ject to our control, that is involved in the Christian
enterprise: it is the whole man.

...God is not taken in by our polite little
speeches. He knows us through and through, far better than we know ourselves. He hears what we are
really saying, he listens to our heart. And if we would
learn to keep company with him, we must become
the kind of people who are prepared to be heard and
addressed at that deep level, which requires a great
deal of honesty and humility....

As long as our religion remains at the level of our
deliberate...personality, it is bound to be a rather on-
and-off affair; if we allow the Lord to get hold of us
at...the heart, below the level of contrivance, then we
have a traitor in the camp! We shall become involved
with God even in spite of ourselves, there will be
something in us undermining our self-built edifice of
conceit and self-will.[5]

God is trying desperately to get in touch with you, at the deepest
level of who you are! He wants to be in an intimate relationship
with you; he wants to know what is going on in your heart. He
actually already knows you better than you know yourself, but for
some strange reason he delights in your telling him, in your relating to him the deep longings of your heart, your dreams, your fears.

Will you respond to him? Will you push through all the cultural clutter around you, push through your own fears and even
pain, to connect with him at that deep level?

I can assure you that this is a journey you will never regret
taking. So stay with me!

THE EBB AND FLOW OF THE SPIRITUAL LIFE

There is a fundamental reality about our spiritual lives that is important to point out before we move on. It's what Saint Ignatius called the experiences of consolation and desolation. These experiences of spiritual closeness and of distance from God are simply parts of the landscape of the spiritual life, and Ignatius points out numerous reasons why both *must* exist in our relationship with the Trinity.

It is perfectly normal to experience times of great closeness to God and then, maybe just days later, deep doubts about whether God even exists. There is a constant back and forth that occurs deep inside us. This "ebb and flow" is part of the journey. It's the very adventure we are called into with God through a life of prayer.

I find that many young adults experience a period of doubt and confusion and just abandon their faith. They don't see the desolation they are experiencing as an opportunity for spiritual growth; they see it as themselves!

Sometimes desolation can be very intense, but no matter how deep it is, it's just a "movement" going through the heart; it's not who we are. And like any other movement going through our hearts on any given day, we can *choose* to go with it or not.

Years after her death there was startling information published about the deep spiritual desolation Mother Teresa experienced for over fifty years. "I am told that God loves me—and yet the reality of darkness & coldness & emptiness is so great that nothing touches my soul."[6] When this news first broke, many atheists and skeptics used it as an opportunity to attack Christianity.

> The atheists of the global village were quick to say "I told you so." They used Teresa's desolation as another proof that believers are deluding themselves.

> Christopher Hitchens...had a simple message...in his
> column in *Newsweek:* God is not great and Teresa is
> not His prophet.
>
> According to Hitchens..., Christianity is a fig-
> ment of the human imagination so powerful that its
> adherents have no eyes to see its flaws, nor ears to
> listen to his refutation. It leads people to believe flat
> contradictions in the very teeth of the evidence.
> Exhibit A in their debunking tirades is Mother Teresa,
> who preached God to others, even though she felt
> racked by doubt herself.[7]

Such conclusions are shallow at best, and they show a clear mis-understanding of the spiritual journey. Mr. Hitchens fails to understand that for those of us who believe, spiritual desolation can be the breeding ground for sainthood.

Many holy people had very desolate periods in their lives. A friend visited Avila, where Saint Teresa lived. His most striking memory was of going into the chapel and seeing a strange collection of tally marks on the wall. The tour guide explained that the marks were made by Teresa herself, during a particularly desolate time in her life. Evidently she would grab a nail hanging on a string outside the chapel entrance and scratch another tally mark into the wall as she entered the chapel for prayer. "Another day you're not here," she would say as she made the mark. She did this every day for over eight years.

John of the Cross, Francis of Assisi, Ignatius of Loyola and many others had experiences of this kind of deep desolation. These are obviously saintly people, yet their prayer lives were marked with significant periods of doubt and confusion. It's just not what you would expect from such holy people.

UNDERSTANDING DESOLATION

Periods of desolation can last for hours, days, weeks, months or even years. Why does God allow us to go through such times of doubt and confusion? We find very clear explanations in the deep riches of Catholic spirituality.

Consolation comes from God and God alone; desolation comes from the enemy and only the enemy. God *never* gives us desolation; however, he will allow the enemy to bring it into our lives.

Saint Ignatius offers three reasons for this spiritual desolation:

> *The first* is because we are tepid, slothful or negligent in our spiritual exercises, and so through our faults spiritual consolation withdraws from us. *The second,* to try us and see how much we are and how much we extend ourselves in his service and praise without so much payment of consolations and increased graces. *The third,* to give us true recognition and understanding so that we may interiorly feel that it is not ours to attain or maintain increased devotion, intense love, tears or any other spiritual consolation, but that all is the gift and grace of God our Lord.[8]

Here we have three simple reasons why desolation occurs: sometimes we bring it on ourselves through sin or other choices; sometimes God allows it to test our resolve—are we in this just for the consolation, to feel close to God, or are we more determined than that; and sometimes God allows it just to make it really clear to us that we can't manufacture consolation on our own. There's nothing we can do to make it happen; it's pure gift, from God alone.

If you take a step back in your own life, I'm sure you will find that your greatest periods of growth have occurred during or shortly after periods of desolation. This is proof that desolation, seen through the lens of Catholic spirituality, is actually a source of *deeper* faith and *stronger* belief.

Imagine if Saint Teresa of Avila had stopped going to the chapel when she had those prolonged feelings that God was nowhere to be found. The testimony to her faith is that she *kept* going, day after day, for more than eight years, feeling every day that God was not even listening!

This is one of the areas of the spiritual life that I believe is in serious need of rearticulation for our times. From my work with young adults, desolation is one of the main stumbling blocks for many. The minute someone experiences some distance from God, it becomes a reason to stop praying and to give up spiritual disciplines. Yet the very purpose of the desolation is to strengthen your resolve, not for you to give up! So hold fast!

I believe the reality of desolation is so crucial an aspect to understand that I'm devoting the next chapter to it. The enemy celebrates many victories as young people get lost in his desolations, so his work is worth analyzing. A detailed breakdown of the enemy and his evil tactics is another great gift Saint Ignatius has given us.

know your enemy

He was home from college, and we got together for coffee. It was nice catching up after he'd been away for the whole semester. For a while it was just small talk, but the conversation eventually got to deeper things. I asked him how his faith life was going. I'm keenly aware that the challenges of college life can sometime cause one to slip.

His response was that things were good. I asked if he had gotten involved in any groups on campus that supported his faith, where he was going to Mass and so on. One answer surprised me: "No, I haven't been going to Mass since the beginning of the semester." I wondered how he could think that his faith life was in a good place.

He told me about the fateful day he stopped going to Mass. He was driving to the Catholic church off campus, which was a bit of a drive. On the way there he kept thinking what a waste of time it was going to this church: The priest was elderly and not very engaging, the people weren't into things at all, the music was horrible. Most Sundays he had trouble even staying awake. Then he had to face the ridicule of friends. And for what?! What did he get out of it?

The closer he got to the church, the more frustrated he felt. So he drove right past the church and out of the little town to a scenic overlook of a national forest. He stopped there and hiked a little way into the woods, to one of the most beautiful scenes of nature he had ever looked at. It was a truly spiritual experience, one that far surpassed any experience he had had the whole semester going to that little church with all those practically dead people.

This young man had been going to "church" in the mountains ever since. Every Sunday he took a hike into nature and spent time alone with God.

As his story went on, I found myself getting more and more uncomfortable. This was going to be a hard conversation. He had a good, convincing argument. He had not only become desolate about his seemingly empty church experience, but he was having what appeared to be a truly spiritual experience outside of church, which seemed to confirm his absence from Mass.

This young man is not alone. There may be many reading this book who have come to the same conclusion he did. But his argument was all wrong. Let's look at the problems with what he was thinking. There are some fundamental truths about himself and the faith that would have helped him navigate the temptation to skip Mass.

THE HIDDEN MIRACLE

First and foremost, what is happening every time we go to Mass, whether we recognize it or not, is absolutely out of this world. The power of the Mass and specifically the miracle of the Eucharist are beyond any human comprehension.

"How can that be?" you say? "It seems so lifeless: The music is terrible, the priest is boring, nobody is singing,..."

But there's a heck of a lot more going on at Mass than what you can see on the surface. A lifeless liturgy doesn't indicate that nothing is happening. Think of the baby Jesus, born to a simple woman in Bethlehem, lying in a manger—basically a food trough for animals. Even though no one could see it, he was the Lord and Creator of the universe! I could give you many examples of this same type of phenomenon: something of great mystical power shrouded in a simple human or earthly form, visible only by faith and only to those open to seeing the spirituality reality.

This all points back to what we talked about in the second chapter: We can't let ourselves get separated from the big story of how God has worked throughout history. He has always hidden himself and left a certain element up to our faith and personal assent. This is a fundamental truth of our faith. If this young man had been rooted in this truth, he wouldn't have so easily given in to the temptation that, if he wasn't "feeling" anything powerful at Mass, then it didn't really matter if he stayed away.

The second problem with the young man's thinking was the conclusion that going off into the woods somewhere was a good substitute for Mass. Such thinking ignores the fundamental reality that we are made for community. As human beings, we were not created for isolation. We were created to enjoy relationship with the heart of Jesus, the heart of God. That reality expresses itself most profoundly in our worship of God.

There is a social element that is fundamental to man's nature—it's part of who we are. Master apologist Frank Sheed said:

> It is not indeed in the nature of man to be an isolated unit all by himself. By his needs and by his powers he is bound up with others. This element too in his nature must be offered to God. The excuse a modern man gives for staying away from Church—that he finds that he prays better alone—misses the point. What he is doing is refusing to join with his fellow men in the worship of God. That is to say, he is leaving the social element in his nature unoffered to God.[1]

Personal quiet times with God are important, and they certainly can occur within the beauty of nature or any environment that fosters depth in your spiritual experience. But such times do not replace at least a weekly participation in the corporate worship of the liturgy. Times of worship with others, particularly the Mass, will fuel the personal times we have with God alone.

THE ENEMY'S TACTICS

At first glance it doesn't seem as if this young man was in a battle, but he truly was, and with a formidable opponent. The real trick in my conversation with him was convincing him of that!

If we want to grow in our experience of prayer, one of the first steps better be to get a clear understanding of who will be opposing us. There *is* an enemy of our spiritual progress, and he will stop at nothing to knock us off track and lead us astray. If we want to have any chance at succeeding in spiritual growth, we need to know not only that there is an enemy but also that he will be ruthless in his attack. We need to know how to sift through his deceptions: He is slick and convincing. He can make what he is trying to sell seem much better than anything our faith has to offer.

The enemy actually is not just the devil: It is defined as the world, the flesh *and* the devil. The enemy of our spiritual journey to God is a powerful, supernatural conspiracy, manipulated and directed by Satan himself. Remember, Saint Ignatius calls him "the enemy of human nature"[2]: He tries to diminish our identity as sons and daughters who give the Father great delight.

Satan takes the allurements and the godlessness of the world, adds our attraction to sin and becomes a force to be reckoned with. He manipulates the temptations sent toward us, tapping into the very things we are drawn to and have a basic susceptibility to because of past experiences. How do we stand a chance?

The thoughts that went through my young friend's head (or heart) on his way to Mass were classic desolation. Remember, desolation is the thoughts, feelings or desires moving at the deepest level of our heart that draw us away from God. A thought about whether or not to go to Mass at first glance may seem fairly superficial. But looked at more closely, we realize that it is one of those deep movements of the heart that definitely impacts our relationship with God.

The thought to skip Mass came from the enemy. With no resistance when it was first thrown out, it was followed by an onslaught of reinforcing thoughts: The priest is old and irrelevant, the music is horrible, the people don't even sing and so on. Before he even knew it, this young man was in an all-out battle and was losing ground fast. By the time he got to the church, it was over—and he hadn't even fought back!

His decision was reinforced by a "spiritual" experience that led to an entire semester of skipping Mass and finding God in nature. That's the way of the enemy. He will deceive us and tempt us with something appealing. That "something" is often a good thing presented as if only he can give it to us. But in reality, the very thing Satan tempts us with is not his anyway. Rather by the very nature of our dignity we already have rights to it.

BASICS OF DISCERNMENT

Once we acknowledge that there *is* an enemy, we have to be able to recognize him when he throws something at us, which will typically happen in our heart. Then we have to fight. Saint Ignatius gives us a strategy for what he calls discernment of spirits, a simple three-step plan: (1) be aware, (2) understand and (3) take action.

First, we have to *be aware* of the activity going on in our heart, especially things happening at the deepest level of our heart. This sometimes requires brutal honesty about what we're thinking, feeling and desiring.

Second, we have to *understand* where those thoughts, feelings or desires are coming from. Are they coming from God, from our own human spirit or from Satan?

The third step is to *take action*. If the movements are from God, receive them and receive them gratefully; if they are not from God, reject them quickly and decisively.

I'm sure that if the young man we have been talking about would have followed this simple three-step plan in the face of his attack, things would have gone very differently. When the first thought hit him: "What a waste of time it is going to Mass," he could have been *aware* of a movement in his heart. After identifying this clearly as a deep, "fundamentally spiritual" thought, feeling or desire, he could have reflected, "Is this from God or not?" Given his Catholic background, he could have quickly *understood* that this was definitely not from God.

Then he could have *taken action* by rejecting the thought quickly and decisively. I would have even encouraged him to do it out loud: "No, I reject this thought, in the name of Jesus. I invite you, Jesus, into this moment of desolation. Renew my desire to meet you in this celebration of the liturgy." He could have added, "I know that it's important for me to go to Mass; there's more going on there than I could ever feel. I *need* the nourishment of the Eucharist to get through this next week. *I am going to Mass!*"

The whole thing would have lasted little more than thirty seconds. He would have found himself at Mass a few minutes later, very likely experiencing a greater outpouring of grace because of his renewed conviction about being there. This is how discernment works. It is very important to understand this activity if we want to grow spiritually.

The cultural dynamics we talked about in chapter two help us understand why this battle is so intense and difficult in a unique way in our times. I don't think that the battle has changed or that the enemy has shifted his tactics. Rather the cultural dynamics have diminished our ability to *be aware* of this spiritual activity.

We're constantly surrounded by noise and distractions that can keep us perpetually focused on the surface, so that we are not aware of the deeper movements going on inside us. Don't be fooled: They are going on, and sometimes they are movements that lead us further away from God without our even realizing it. We are uniquely vulnerable to these attacks because of the diminished capacity for intimacy that our culture engenders.

If we desire to grow in our prayer, we must strengthen our "muscles" of spiritual discernment. We must allow the Lord to love us intimately and make us more aware of the activity constantly going on within and around us.

OTHER DESOLATE DECISIONS

I met with a young woman the other day. We spent quite a bit of time just catching up, because it had been a while since we had seen each other. In time the conversation moved to spiritual things, as I asked what God was doing in her life.

For the next several minutes this woman shared about how distant she had grown in her faith over the past year or so. She explained how alone she felt and how sometimes it seemed as if she was the only person she knew who even believed in God, how God seemed so far away, as if he never was there. She knew she had had experiences of his working in her life, but she couldn't remember any of them. She became very emotional as she shared these deep feelings of desolation.

It all hit a culmination when she said, "How can God be real when so many people don't even believe in him?"

In that statement, I believe, we hit the deep desolation that she was experiencing. Unfortunately, it had been going on for months and had led her to all sorts of decisions about her spiritual life: She wasn't praying anymore, she was frequently missing Sunday Mass, and she was not having fellowship with any other believers on a regular basis. Now she found herself struggling to hold ground on a number of moral matters that in the past had not been issues for her.

She related how much she desired to be connected to God and to her faith, but when it came to doing anything about it, she just didn't do it. It's no wonder that she felt as if she had lost her faith. I cried with her as she shared, because I could relate with this deep feeling.

This is classic desolation. It is evident even in some of the wording of her emotions: never, always, no one, the only person. This is the voice of the enemy: He tends to speak in absolutes like this.

The desolation didn't happen overnight; the enemy can be very patient. He is willing to very subtly feed us one line after another, as long as we're willing to take them, for as long as it takes to lead us astray. He is a ruthless enemy who "prowls around like a roaring lion, seeking some one to devour" (1 Peter 5:8). We can never afford to let our guard down. Any chink in the armor or slight breech in the wall, he will seek to exploit. But what can we do, practically, in the face of his attacks?

I shared with this young woman some fundamentals about desolation, many of the things we have talked about in this chapter. Her story offers a unique opportunity to review what we have discussed and to offer some further insights into this topic.

RULES FOR DISCERNMENT

Fortunately, Saint Ignatius offers fourteen rules for discernment of spirits that can help us immensely in this battle against the enemy. Always remember, though, that this is not a battle we are fighting on our own. If we approach it like that, we will lose before we even begin.

This is a battle that *Jesus* is fighting for us, and we are constantly inviting him to take up the fight on our behalf. He has already won this victory, once and for all. Now Jesus' Spirit speaks within our hearts, to have us enjoy the fullness of our spiritual inheritance as coheirs with him! We need to learn to receive all that is ours in Jesus' heart and to fight evil as Jesus did. When we do we will taste his victory and his love as realities in our own life.

Here's a basic breakdown of Saint Ignatius' fourteen rules:

▸▸ Rules 1 and 2 talk of the person moving from bad to worse and the person moving from good to better.[3] These are "the two fundamental directions of the spiritual life": (1) "*away from God* and *toward serious sin*" and (2) "*toward God* and *away from serious sin*."[4] Notice that there isn't a middle ground where you can be on vacation. You're either making progress or losing ground.

▸▸ Rule 3 defines what consolation is and how we experience it.

▸▸ Rule 4 defines what desolation is and how we experience it.

▸▸ Rule 5 instructs that in times of desolation we are never to make a change in our spiritual discipline, in our vocation or direction in life.

▸▸ Rule 6 tells us specifically what is helpful in times of desolation: prayer, meditation, much examination and some suitable form of penance.

▸▸ Rule 7 encourages us to think of desolation as a "trial" permitted by the Lord.

▸▸ Rule 8 teaches that desolation is a time for patience.

▸▸ Rule 9 gives the three reasons for desolation: our own spiritual negligence, to try us and to give us true recognition that all is the gift and grace of God our Lord.

▸▸ Rule 10 teaches that consolation is a time for preparation.

▸▸ Rule 11 tells us the attitudes we should have in consolation (humility) and in desolation (confidence).

▸▸ Rules 12 through 14 give the specific tactics of the enemy when desolation crystallizes into a temptation.

APPLYING THE RULES

I talk with many young people who are experiencing periods of great desolation and have no idea why. They have simply resigned themselves to feeling desolate, and they gradually abandon their daily spiritual habits. After a period of time, they find themselves in a faith crisis.

Look to Rule 5, I tell them: In a time of desolation, *never* make a change. Don't stop praying, don't stop going to Mass, don't stop spending time with friends who support you in your faith.

Every temptation you can imagine will come into your mind to abandon these things, but make no changes. Train yourself, that in those times when you are feeling distant from God, it is just not an option to change anything that you were already doing to grow in your spiritual life. You are meant to enjoy Jesus' victory over all sin and death and to live in intimate love with him.

Then look to Rule 6. A time of desolation is a time for initiative, for action. And there are very specific things you can do:

1. *Pray.* Ask God to take the desolation away and return his consolation to you; ask him for strength to persevere in this time of desolation, and ask him for clarity to know why the desolation has come to you.
2. *Meditate.* Recall past times of consolation, past times of closeness with God in prayer or otherwise, times when you have especially felt God's love for you.
3. *Examine* (take note that this is the *third* step; it should not happen before the first two). With God's help and revelation and with inspired confidence, calling to mind past times of consolation, ask God to reveal to you the source of this desolation. There are only three reasons for desolation, as described in Rule 9.

4. *Extend* yourself in some suitable form of penance. This is a tangible thing you can do to make your rejection of the desolation firm and real to you. It doesn't have to be a big thing. If you had planned on praying for thirty minutes, pray those thirty minutes, then pray another two minutes. This is a simple way of extending yourself in the *direction* of God, resisting the temptation and the *direction* of the desolation.

Approaching this topic is a big task, one that I can't do full justice to in this book. It's critical, I believe, to have a clear understanding that there *is* an enemy and that his primary activity is to prevent our spiritual growth. I encourage you to learn more, so that you will be able to relate to the love of the Holy Spirit, who has us taste what Jesus does in an ongoing, heart-to-heart conversation with the Father.

One book that has helped me immensely is *The Discernment of Spirits: An Ignatian Guide for Everyday Living* by Father Timothy Gallagher. Father Gallagher's treatment of the rules for discernment is both insightful and contemporary. I find his explanations very practical and down-to-earth, with many examples from real people struggling through the same issues I face in my own life. I highly recommend it.

prayer principles

I have made numerous comments so far about my spiritual director, Father Scott Traynor. He is an amazing priest and a good friend who has had a significant impact on my life. Much of the content in this book is to the credit of the spiritual formation I have received from him. This formation has given me new words to understand and express what I experience in prayer.

In this chapter I wish to convey some of that new language, as best I can. I find myself thinking about these things a lot. I've developed charts and diagrams and maps.

Now, some of my close friends make fun of my pictures and concentric circles, but please bear with me as I share this with you. I have found this new understanding quite liberating in my prayer life, and I hope that it will draw you into a greater experience of intimacy with the Lord in prayer.

MEASURES OF PRAYER

When you start something it's important not only to set a goal but to define that goal. The same is true for the spiritual journey. If I am going to try to get better at prayer, what is that going to look like? How will I know when I'm there?

These are great questions and ones that I believe don't get asked very often. If they did, there would be greater clarity about what exactly good prayer looks like, and more people would be getting there.

Ultimately the goal is heaven. But what about before we get there? Until then, I believe the goal we are shooting for is to pray well.

So what measures "good" prayer? How can you tell if someone is good at it?

Many saints have recorded very powerful, even mystical experiences with God in prayer. We think of Saint Teresa of Avila and Saint John of the Cross as good prayers. But is mystical experience the measure? It can't be, for two reasons.

First, holy people don't have these experiences all the time. We've already talked about the fact that some of them have had very prolonged and intense periods of desolation. It would be silly to conclude that somehow during these periods of desolation they became bad at prayer.

Second, when the saints did have powerful experiences, these experiences came not from them but from God. These holy men and women couldn't manufacture the mystical experience. God gave it to them; it was pure gift.

Maybe the measure would be the spiritual gifts the person has? We have all kinds of stories of holy men and women who had very powerful spiritual gifts: the gift of reading souls in confession, the gift of healing or miracles, prophetic gifts and so on. But this couldn't be the measure either, for the same reason as the first. These people had nothing to do with the gifts they had. God gave them the gifts, to be used in the building of his kingdom. Take any one of these people, no matter how holy, and if they started using their gifts for their own purposes or for some other reason than for what God intended, the gift would cease to operate in them. God gave the gift, God held it in operation, and the use of the gift was dependent on him and his power.

We could keep speculating about possibilities, but let's get to the point. If we're going to define a measure for good prayer, it would have to be a measure of what we actually contribute. And the only things we bring to the equation of prayer are showing up and being real—consistency and honesty. We have to show up for prayer to happen, and when we show up, we need to be honest about what's going on in our hearts.

As we discussed earlier, prayer is all about a relationship. No one can sustain a relationship without honesty and consistency. If you hardly spend any time together, and if you're not honest with each other when you are together, I'm not sure what you would call it, but you couldn't call it a relationship. Yet many of us approach our prayer life like this. We hardly spend any time with God, we vacillate in our commitment to prayer at the slightest hint of desolation, and when we actually do pray, we try to present to God this image of ourselves that we think he wants to see, as if we can hide our real selves from him.

Consistency and honesty are the two key measures of prayer. Let's look a little more closely at each.

CONSISTENCY AND HONESTY

Prayer is a relationship, and no relationship will last without time together. If you desire to grow in your faith life, you *must* make a commitment to consistently spend time in prayer. There is no other way.

At first this may seem a burden; at times you may even doubt whether you should be praying when your heart is so *not* into it. But I guarantee you, if you push through those times and pray anyway, your reward will be great!

I shared my own experience coming to this conviction back in chapter one. I still struggle at times with consistency, but I am definitely convinced that I don't operate as well when I am not praying every day. I miss that time with the Lord and how it guides me, even when God doesn't seem particularly close to me or prayer seems dry. Prayer has become a bit of a routine in my life, and when I miss the routine, something feels out of whack throughout my day.

Many people struggle with consistent prayer, but with a little perseverance you can get on the other side of the curve, where the consistent times are more frequent than the inconsistent times, where you pray more days than you miss. This is the kind of consistency I am talking about. Make a commitment to spend time every day in prayer. I guarantee that the return on your investment will far outweigh anything else you are doing with your time.

The other measure for prayer is honesty. There are several facets to this that need to be addressed.

First, in prayer we need to be honest with God about what's going on in our hearts. Prayer needs to be real, not some pretense or act. God already knows everything about us: He knows us better than we know ourselves. What could we possibly hide from him?

Second, in order to be honest with God about what's going on in our hearts, we have to know. We have to be aware of the movements going on there, especially those that are moving on the deepest level (see chapter three). This is the stuff of real prayer: honest, straight from the heart, sometimes even gut-wrenching sharing. This is what God is looking for. His deepest desire is to be in intimate relationship with us, as we truly are.

These two measures of prayer give us something that we can actually shoot for. Anyone can show up—be committed to spending time in prayer. And though it's a little more challenging, we all are capable of getting in touch with what's moving in our hearts and then being honest about what we find there.

I don't know about you, but when I learned this, I was inspired. In all the years I struggled with dissatisfaction with a mediocre prayer life, I always chalked it up to something being wrong with me. Maybe I just didn't have what it takes to be holy, I thought, or maybe I just didn't know enough for my prayer to be effective. I kept buying books and trying new approaches. But when I found out that the two things that measured prayer were two things I knew I could deliver, that pumped me up.

In your prayer these are two things that *you* can deliver too: consistency and honesty. How simple can it get?

ESSENTIAL DYNAMICS OF PRAYER

With the measures for prayer clear, we can look at the dynamics of prayer itself. Simply put, they are *acknowledge, relate, receive* and *respond*. These are the dynamics of prayer because they're the dynamics of any relationship.

Think of any close friend you are in a relationship with. These dynamics pretty much capture what goes on between you. You *acknowledge* some movement in your heart about the other person or about something else you care deeply about; you *relate* that movement or feeling to the person; you in turn *receive* from the other person, which typically stirs something in you, to which you *respond*. It's sort of like a good dance, knowing where to move and when.

If you have ever experienced a deep conversation with a close friend, think back to what transpired, and I think you will find these dynamics. You share, the other person listens and shares, you listen, and so on. The whole thing goes off track when one friend fails to really hear what the other is saying.

Have you ever had one of those experiences where someone really isn't listening? You can almost see the person thinking about what to say once you stop talking. Those kinds of experiences usually cause us to shut down and disengage. Once you skip a step in these fundamental dynamics of relationship, the conversation ceases to be.

In prayer the relationship is with God—Father, Son and Holy Spirit.

▶▶ First we get in touch with what is moving in our hearts, particularly at the deepest level—*acknowledge.*

▶▶ Second, we *relate* those movements to God in prayer.

▶▶ Third, we listen and *receive* whatever he desires to give us in response to what we shared.

▶▶ Finally, we *respond* to what we just received, which is typically a natural movement, not something forced or burdensome.

Level 1
Surface Feelings, Thoughts, Desires

Level 2
Fundamentally Psychological Feelings, Thoughts, Desires
• Psychological Consolations
• Psychological Desolations

Influenced by:
Family Relationships • Sexual Desires • Ethnic Temperaments • DNA • Deep Moods • Cultural Assumptions
(e.g., money, beauty, customs, myths, ethos, etc.)

Pleasure/Pain Principle

Level 3
Fundamentally Spiritual
• Spiritual Consolations
• Spiritual Desolations
• Affective Movements = Spirits

Intellect   Emotion   Will
(thoughts) (feelings) (choices)

Imagination/Memories

Indwelling Holy Spirit

Because these essential dynamics are the defining marks of any relationship, they should be present in your prayer life, no matter how you pray. There are many different methods or styles of prayer: Liturgy of the Hours, Marian prayer, scriptural prayer and so on. But no matter which method you use, these dynamics will, or should, be present in all of them.

These dynamics don't define a new method; they simply articulate the flow or movement of the relationship. Any method of prayer should draw us into a deeper relationship with the Trinity. If it isn't doing that for us, then we're not using the method properly.

I can remember times in my prayer journey when my relationship with Mary was a particular focus. During those times the rosary was a main staple of my prayer. At other times I found great grace in praying the Liturgy of the Hours. But what was often missing for me during these times was the relationship. I became so focused on the method that I lost sight of what the method was supposed to be leading me to. Something would move deeply within me—some new insight or deep emotion. But my thoughts would quickly return to the method I was using. What I should have done in those moments was stop and listen. I had connected with God, which is exactly the purpose of prayer.

This is very much like being in a conversation with another person and shutting off the person's response, pushing through with whatever I was saying. It would be a somewhat one-sided relationship. This may be a form of prayer, and it can still contribute to our growth toward holiness, but it does not allow the Lord to address us at the level of the heart, as we discussed in chapter three.

THE CENTRALITY OF RECEPTIVITY

Allowing the Lord to touch us at the level of the heart is *the* key to prayer. As I have grown in my own prayer life the past several years, I have found this to be true. My spiritual director is constantly saying to me, "Receive, receive, receive!"

Sometimes when I think I have received all there is to receive, I am surprised to find out there is more. Through a series of questions from my spiritual director, or from my wife if I am sharing with her what God is doing in my prayer, a whole area of inter-pretation that I never even considered becomes clear to me.

In our culture we have a tendency toward the immediate. We want things quickly and with little effort. This is one effect of the culture that we have to shake off, because it is just not conducive to prayer.

Some of the most powerful experiences I have had in the past several years have occurred after pushing through sometimes weeks of seeming nothingness. I would reflect long and hard on an image I felt God had brought to me in prayer. I would try to "milk" the image for all it was worth, engaging my imagination and all my senses, really praying that I would get all that the Lord wanted me to. And finally one day it would all break open, and this flood of insight and revelation would occur.

I truly believe those experiences would have never happened had I not waited on God and kept the image or experience before me until God was done. Often I had had enough of the image weeks before, but I knew God wasn't done showing me something.

Saint Francis de Sales describes such experiences: "If your mind finds enough appeal, light, and fruit in any of them, remain with that point and do not go on any further. Imitate the bees, who do not leave a flower as long as they can extract any honey out of it."[1]

Being open, being receptive, is key. In fact it is so critical that we shouldn't depend on our own ability for it.

Father Scott has counseled me to pray constantly that God would expand my capacity to receive. It is a prayer that I have said often over the past few years. "Lord, help me to receive even more of you than I am capable of receiving; open me up, enlarge the ter-ritory within me, expand me! Expand my capacity to receive you."

And this is a prayer that is not just a part of my daily prayer time; it's one I lift up all the time, throughout my day. In fact, I also have made it a constant prayer for my wife, for my kids and for the other youth ministers and teens that I work with. I find it to be a powerful prayer; I have been amazed at the ways God has answered it in very tangible ways.

When you think about participating in "real" prayer, remember that we as creatures can only *receive* from God: Everything comes from him. To grow in our willingness and ability to receive ultimately determines the quality and growth of our prayer—our relationship with the Father, Son and Holy Spirit.

THE ROAD TO EMMAUS: A SCHOOL OF PRAYER

That very day two of them were going to a village named Emmaus, about seven miles from Jerusalem, and talking with each other about all these things that had happened. While they were talking and discussing together, Jesus himself drew near and went with them. But their eyes were kept from recognizing him. And he said to them, "What is this conversation which you are holding with each other as you walk?" And they stood still, looking sad. Then one of them, named Cleopas, answered him, "Are you the only visitor to Jerusalem who does not know the things that have happened there in these days?" And he said to them, "What things?" And they said to him, "Concerning Jesus of Nazareth, who was a prophet mighty in deed and word before God and all the people, and how our chief priests and rulers delivered him up to be condemned to death, and crucified him. But we had hoped that he was the one to redeem Israel. Yes, and besides all this, it is now the third day since this happened. Moreover, some women of our company amazed us. They were at the tomb early in the morning and did not find his body;

and they came back saying that they had even seen a vision of angels, who said that he was alive. Some of those who were with us went to the tomb, and found it just as the women had said; but him they did not see. And he said to them, "O foolish men, and slow of heart to believe all that the prophets have spoken! Was it not necessary that the Christ should suffer these things and enter into his glory?" And beginning with Moses and all the prophets, he interpreted to them in all the Scriptures the things concerning himself.

So they drew near to the village to which they were going. He appeared to be going further, but they constrained him, saying, "Stay with us, for it is toward evening and the day is now far spent." So he went in to stay with them. When he was at table with them, he took the bread and blessed and broke it, and gave it to them. And their eyes were opened and they recognized him; and he vanished out of their sight. They said to each other, "Did not our hearts burn within us while he talked to us on the road, while he opened to us the Scriptures?" And they rose that same hour and returned to Jerusalem; and they found the Eleven gathered together and those who were with them, who said, "The Lord has risen indeed, and has appeared to Simon!" Then they told what had happened on the road, and how he was known to them in the breaking of the bread. (Luke 24:13–35)

There are a number of passages in Scripture that we could call "schools of prayer"—passages that teach the essential dynamics of prayer through the real-life experiences of the people in those times. The story of the road to Emmaus is one of those passages.

Let's set the stage a little: We have here two disciples, very disheartened by recent events, having decided to go back home. All that they had hoped for over the past weeks (months, years?) had been lost. They were returning to what they knew.

Notice how the essential dynamics of prayer play out throughout the rest of this passage.

The disciples were pretty much in touch with what was going on in their hearts (*acknowledge*); it's all they were talking about. Suddenly Jesus was walking with them, "but their eyes were kept from recognizing him." As they walked along, Jesus asked them what they were talking about. "Are you the only visitor to Jerusalem who does not know the things that have happened there in these days?" was their reply. "What things?" Jesus asked.

Was he serious? If there was anyone who knew very intimately what had gone on in Jerusalem, it was Jesus. It all happened to him. Yet Jesus knew that the disciples needed to share what was going on in their hearts.

Their explanation wasn't very neat. Jesus, a prophet, mighty in deed and word, was delivered up to death by the chief priests and rulers; we had hoped that he was the one to redeem Israel; now it's the third day since all this happened; some women amazed us, for they went to the tomb and didn't find his body; some angels said he was alive; other people went to the tomb and found it just as the women had said, but him they did not see.

What a bundle of thoughts, feelings and desires: affection, hope, dashed hope, anger, sadness, grief, disillusionment, confusion, faint new hope but lack of trust. These disciples related what was there, in all its messiness. They poured their hearts out (*relate*) in one big dump.

Then, because they honestly related what was going on inside their hearts, particularly things at the deepest level, they were naturally poised to *receive*. And look at what they received! Probably one of the greatest Bible studies of all time: "Beginning with Moses and all the prophets, [Jesus] interpreted to them in all the Scriptures the things concerning himself. "It was such a powerful experience that they later would reflect on how their hearts were burning inside them as they listened to all that he shared.

And in typical fashion with "receive, receive, receive," the disciples couldn't get enough. When they drew near the village, Jesus appeared to be continuing his journey, so they *related* their intense desire to stay with him, they then *received* more of him as he complied with their request and stayed to share a meal with them. This passage is a beautiful example of the dance of these relational dynamics.

Finally we see the disciples *responding* to all that happened to them. It wasn't a burdensome response; it flowed very naturally from what they had received. They rose "at that same hour," which was at night, and ran seven miles back to Jerusalem. I'm sure they weren't complaining the whole way about how hard this was; they were far too excited about relating all that had happened to the other disciples.

When speaking about this fourth dynamic, *respond*, my spiritual director often uses the image of a sailboat. The boat doesn't do anything burdensome to respond to the wind in its sail—it simply moves forward, propelled by the wind. Turning the sail into the wind is receptivity, catching all that the wind has to offer to expand the sail to its capacity. The sailboat responds by moving forward, but it is the wind that is carrying it.

Our response to God in prayer should be a natural movement, a natural response to what we have *received*, not some task or chore we make up for ourselves. Our response is some form of personal version of Mary's yes, "Let it be to me according to your word" (Luke 1:38).

The Emmaus passage gives us a great lived experience of the relational dynamics of prayer—acknowledge, relate, receive, respond—which is why we call it a school of prayer. I encourage you to use it in your own prayer. Enter into the passage, imagine yourself there with the two disciples, walking along the road. See what the Lord has for you as you "make new" the event through the gift of prayer.

short circuits and how to fix them

I met with a young adult for coffee one day. He had spent the summer serving with a missionary group, and he was still flying high from his amazing experience of ministry. He told me that he had grown in his prayer life during this time. Obviously, this was something I was very excited to hear about.

He had been going to Mass every day, and his ministry team had prayed the Liturgy of the Hours together all summer, four or five times a day! He had also prayed the rosary daily with another team member, with whom he had become close friends. All in all, he had put in more time in prayer than he ever had in his life.

This new love of prayer sounded great. I asked him what God had been showing him in all this time he had been spending with him. The young man, genuinely confused, asked what I meant. I tried to explain prayer as a relationship. In all this new time he was spending, surely God was talking to him, revealing something to him?

The man's response was quick, which led me to believe that it was authentic, "Oh, that's the one type of prayer I'm not very good at—reflective prayer. Every time I try to get quiet and listen, I just can't get rid of all the distractions."

I wasn't sure how to proceed. Here was this incredible young man who just had the summer of a lifetime and felt closer to God than ever before. Yet what he was experiencing in prayer was not all that there was. In fact, I believe that he was just scratching the surface, not really experiencing the deep intimacy that the Lord was offering him.

I finally asked him if there was something keeping him from being intimate with God in prayer. As much as I tried not to, my question seemed to cast doubt on his feelings of closeness with God. So to help him understand, I talked about my relationship with my wife.

I had him imagine that I suddenly had this period of months when I had more time than ever to spend with my wife. I love her very much, and time is often our greatest poverty. But suppose, after months of this, a friend asked me, "So what's happening in your relationship with all this newfound time? What's moving between you?" If my answer to that question was, "What do you mean?" or, "I don't understand," my friend would think that there was something seriously wrong with me. How could I possibly be spending so much time with my wife and not have things happen in the relationship, not have "new stuff" move in my heart and between us?

There was a long period of silence, the kind that I have learned to wait through in situations like these. Eventually my young friend looked at me, with tears in his eyes, and said, "I don't think I can trust God like that."

Wow! There was a powerful moment. For the first time, I think, this young man came face-to-face with one of his deepest fears: whether or not he could trust people and, more importantly, whether or not he could trust God.

There was much more conversation after this, and many other conversations after that one. Eventually there was even time for us to pray together for healing of that lack of trust, which all stemmed back to a very broken relationship with his father.

This story helps convey the point of the last chapter, while at the same time transitioning into the content of this chapter. All of the things we have talked about so far—the measures of prayer and the essential dynamics of prayer—have to work in harmony. When we consistently and honestly relate our thoughts, feelings and desires to God, especially those at the deepest level of our heart, it naturally puts us in a place to *receive* what he wants to give or share with us. We then make our focus to receive *all* that he is offering—receive, receive, receive. This generous receptivity naturally disposes us to *respond* out of the context of our relationship and what we have received.

But when any one of these measures or dynamics gets overemphasized or underemphasized, we experience what we could call a "short circuit" in our prayer. Our prayer is not having us fall more and more in love with God as it is meant to.

In the example I just shared, that young man had a very strong emphasis on consistency, even quantity, but very little honesty. I don't think he was being dishonest purposefully; he wasn't even aware of any deep feelings inside him. If you look closely at the feeling he eventually expressed, though, it was clearly at the deepest level of his heart. But because he was not even aware of it, how could he honestly relate it to God in prayer?

His prayer, though frequent, was not really leading him to deeper intimacy with the Lord. It had benefits, but it was not fulfilling God's deepest desire for him.

That day in the coffee shop, when he was able to say for the first time, "I don't think I can trust you, God," is when God really got him at the level of the heart. And *that* is real prayer.

SHORT CIRCUITS

Please don't misunderstand me here. I'm not saying that this young man's prayer all summer was to no avail. In fact, it was very likely the time he spent in prayer over those couple months that disposed him to what happened with me that day and eventually to the experience of significant healing in his life. He may not have been able to tap into that awareness had he not been praying as much as he was.

There's a certain quality to God's life and to time spent with him: It's called "efficacious." Simply put, this means that grace, without destroying human freedom, at the same time is not dependent upon the human will to accomplish its intended effect. There *are* benefits to time spent in prayer, even when we are not connecting at the level of the heart.

What I am pointing out here, though, is an avoidance of intimacy. God is attempting to connect with you, but you avoid him, whether intentionally or not. It may be the result of a lack of awareness, the result of shallowness, the result of fear or any number of things. The point is, the free flow of grace has somehow been compromised, or worse, cut off altogether.

A short circuit in electrical appliances causes the flow of electricity to be diverted from its intended path. The same is true in prayer. When a short circuit happens, the flow of energy gets diverted from what God intended and toward something else.

There are a number of ways that this happens, and because short circuits almost always occur during the dynamic of receptivity, it's critical to discuss them with as much clarity as possible.

No Interior Life

One obvious short circuit to prayer is the inability to be aware of yourself "on the inside." The ancient Greek maxim "Know thyself" lends itself well here. Our prayer journey is one that takes place in the heart. If we aren't aware of what is going on in our hearts, if we don't know ourselves, we're going to have a very difficult time praying with any effectiveness.

And that knowledge is not just on the positive side. Part of our self-awareness needs to be a clear understanding of what we're *not* and what we *don't have.* We are creatures, in desperate need of our Creator, yet we often live as if we don't depend on him at all. That is a clear indicator of a lack of self-awareness. We are not sufficient, and there is nothing we can do to fill the void within us: Only God can do that.

Many factors contribute to this inability to be "interior" with ourselves. The world around us offers little opportunity for quiet and reflection. The pace of our life, the constant noise in our environment, the barrage of media and images—all contribute to a poverty of silence, which is the breeding ground of the interior life. Years of this rapid, noisy pace leave us somewhat impaired, sort of "attention deficit," when it comes to prayer. We have a difficult time quieting ourselves, stilling our hearts and listening.

If your life is constantly filled with noise and activity, I want to encourage you, even challenge you, to take time to be silent. Your prayer life requires it; *you* need it. You will be amazed at how much more peaceful you will be if you are committed to taking time every day to just be quiet. It won't come naturally at first; it may even require a *lot* of effort to be silent for even ten or fifteen minutes. But I have found it to be a skill that grows over time. Keep pushing, and the "muscles" of reflection will grow as they are used.

The "Self-Help" Syndrome

Check out any bookstore, and you will find entire sections devoted to self-help books. I am often blown away by the many different approaches to fixing ourselves. Our culture is permeated with this mentality of analysis and introspection.

The whole approach is "fixing" and "figuring out." Well, I have good news for us all: We don't have to fix ourselves! That was never what God intended, and the Scriptures and the Church speak to this reality. We are not meant to change ourselves; in fact, we *can't*. Jesus did that, once and for all. "For our sake [God] made him to be sin who knew no sin, so that in him we might become the righteousness of God" (2 Corinthians 5:21; see also Galatians 2:20; Colossians 1:24–27; *CCC*, 521). And he invites us to cooperate with the grace that he offers. That grace is his very life inside us, moving in us, working in us, changing us from the inside out.

The self-help syndrome is one of the most common short circuits to our prayer. The activity can seem spiritual, and that's why it's so dangerous.

I can give you an example from my own experience. I have five children, several of them little ones. At times I feel as if I'm going to pull the hair right out of my head. I get frustrated, especially when I can't get my children to respond. I'm all for crazy, wild and fun, but come on, sometimes you've got to focus and get done whatever you need to do. Bedtime is usually the craziest, with kids running wild, it seems, all over the house.

There have been times when my reaction to all this chaos was to just blow up. After asking nine or ten times, with increasing volume, but to no avail, I resorted to maniacal anger.

I brought this problem to prayer many times. I related my anger to God, told him about how frustrated I was with the lack of response from the kids, how crazy it made me feel at times. So I acknowledged what was moving in my heart; I honestly related it to God.

At first it may not seem as if this is a movement at the deepest level of my heart, but it is. Remember, movements at the deepest level of the heart are those that impact our relationship with God and with carrying out his will. Carrying out his will in my life is intimately connected with the fact that I am a husband and a father: That's my primary vocation; it's part of who I am. So this deep anger with my children, who are also intimately connected to my identity, was a feeling at the deepest level of my heart.

Once I honestly related it to God, then I waited for his response; I waited to receive.

I had this thought in my mind that what I needed was patience. It made me think of the fruits of the Holy Spirit, so I would open my Bible to Galatians 5 and read the list of fruits that Paul gives. It would convict me even more: Yes, what I needed was more patience. So I would return to prayer: "Lord, give me more patience; help me in those moments with the kids to be calm, to not lose my temper. Holy Spirit, give me more of the fruit of patience."

It all sounds so spiritual, and before meeting Father Scott, I was convinced that I was doing exactly what I should. But it *never* worked. I found myself within the next several days in the exact same pattern: getting angry with the kids, losing my temper and going back to pray for more patience.

I was using a self-help approach to Christianity. I would diagnose myself and then, like a good doctor, prescribe myself a prescription: patience. Then I went to God and told him to fill the prescription. Is it any wonder that nothing ever changed? The language itself is all wrong. Anytime we find ourselves telling God what to do, we're in trouble.

At the very center of this self-help approach was *me*. It was all about figuring me out and fixing myself. This is a direct prod-uct of our culture. And just like our bankrupt culture, the approach was empty. I *can't* fix myself, and I can't even begin to figure myself out, so the end result was a hopeless feeling of futility. And that's a surefire short circuit to prayer.

But this is not the life that Jesus is inviting us into. If this is your experience of prayer, I have good news: There's another way to live!

ANOTHER WAY TO LIVE

God's answer is to let Jesus be the center of everything. Read that passage in Colossians 1:24–27 again. The whole mystery of our faith is what? Christ *in* us, "the hope of glory." The self-help approach is one of Christ *and* you, but that's not what the verse says.

The reality is that none of us can live this Christian life, not one. But the hope is that there *is* one who did, and his name is Jesus. God's plan throughout salvation history was to put the life of the one who *did* live the Christian life, and is still living it, into the lives of those who *can't*–us. God doesn't want you to live the Christian life; if that's what you think the invitation is, you've got it all wrong. He wants Jesus to live the Christian life *in* you! And through Jesus you are to become the very righteousness of God (2 Corinthians 5:21).

With a new understanding of living a different way, with Jesus at the center, here's what my prayer looks like today: I acknowledge my anger and honestly relate it to God, just as before. Then I wait and focus on being receptive, even praying that God would help me be more receptive. I avoid the temptation to diagnose myself or figure things out and instead focus on letting God reveal himself to me.

Waiting on God can take a little time, but eventually I experience his response. One time it was a question in my mind: "Why am I angry?"

I remembered that Father Scott had said that most anger is rooted in fear. So the first question quickly led to a second, "Is there something I'm afraid of?"

I was particularly concerned with not analyzing, not trying to figure things out. So I very consciously prayed, "Lord, I don't want to try to figure anything out here. I want to be open to your revelation and your healing. If there is something I am fearful of, please show me."

What happened next was really beautiful. There was a long period of silence. My mind was really empty; I even started to think that maybe God didn't have anything to say. I could have short-circuited the whole thing again if I hadn't pushed through and waited.

But after maybe ten minutes of quiet, this very simple thought went through my mind: "You're not a bad dad."

At first I was confused. I thought to myself, "I know I'm not a bad dad. What does this have to do with my anger?"

But the thought came again: "You're not a bad dad."

And it started to settle into my heart. I had an image of one of those chaotic moments, with my kids running all around me, seemingly out of control. I heard myself say, "Why won't they listen to me? Why can't I get them in control? What am I doing wrong?"

Suddenly this fear deep inside me surfaced. I was scared to death that somehow I was going to fail as a father. I prayed, "Lord, I invite you into this fear. You're in me, so you know it well. I desire your revelation and healing in this area of my life. I desire to surrender everything to you, even this deep fear within me."

I suddenly had an image in my mind of my father. My relationship with my dad was never very close. For whatever reason, there were some things that I was just not able to get from him, particularly his approval. I always felt that I didn't measure up. But my dad died years ago, and I know that his approval is something he can't give me anymore. Yet I was aware of this intense desire to please him, to hear his approval of me.

I didn't get where God was going with all this. Then the image of my father was replaced with an image of Jesus being baptized by John the Baptist. As the whole scene came alive in my imagination, I saw the clouds rent and the skies opened up, almost as if I was actually standing there. Then I heard the words, "This is my beloved Son, with whom I am well pleased" (Matthew 3:17).

As I heard those words, the whole image changed. Suddenly I was the one being baptized by John the Baptist. God showed me that *he* is my Father, he affirms me, he approves me, he validates my worth. And he saves me from a self-centeredness that believes I can "diagnose" and "fix" myself.

Do you see the two ways to live here? The exact same situation was prayed through in two very different ways. The first had pretty mediocre and eventually only negative results; the second is this incredible experience of God's revealing more about myself to me and then bringing healing to me in the very area he was revealing to me.

This second way to live, with Jesus at the center, is marked by truths and affirmations, not by questions, introspection and analysis. It's marked by God's revelation and healing, not by fixing and figuring out. This way of living is marked by the experience of unconditional love, with God informing and inspiring our identity.

NEW WINE

On the third day there was a marriage at Cana in Galilee, and the mother of Jesus was there; Jesus also was invited to the marriage, with his disciples. When the wine failed, the mother of Jesus said to him, "They have no wine." And Jesus said to her, "O woman, what have you to do with me? My hour has not yet come." His mother said to the servants, "Do whatever he tells you." Now six stone jars were standing there, for the Jewish rites of purification, each holding twenty or thirty gallons. Jesus said to them, "Fill the jars with water." And they filled them up to the brim. He said to them, "Now draw some out, and take it to the steward of the feast." So they took it. When the steward of the feast tasted the water now become wine, and did not know where it came from (though the servants who had drawn the water knew), the steward of the feast called the bridegroom and said to him, "Every man serves the good wine first; and when men have drunk freely, then the poor wine; but you have kept the good wine until now." This, the first of his signs, Jesus did at Cana in Galilee, and manifested his glory; and his disciples believed in him. (John 2:1–11)

This is a popular passage. Many of us have heard it before. Have you ever wondered why the couple never asked Jesus to help them? It's not a question I ever thought of until Father Scott asked it. But it provides a great ending to this chapter.

The Gospel tells us that this was "the first" of Jesus' miracles. So maybe the couple didn't know who Jesus was, or if they did, they didn't believe that asking him would make any difference. Or maybe it just didn't occur to them to ask; they would figure out the problem on their own. Or maybe they didn't want to bother him, especially with something as trivial as wine. Or maybe they didn't feel worthy of his help.

These possible reasons are very similar to our own reasons for not approaching Jesus. We find ourselves in periods of doubt or unbelief, we struggle trying to fix things on our own, or we struggle with our worthiness before the Lord. The point is, *none* of these reasons are good reasons, and each of them is rooted in some untruth, some fundamental misunderstanding of *who* Jesus is.

At every moment he desires to love us, in and through all of creation. He is always open to us, always inviting, always receptive. No matter how insignificant our worries seem to us, he welcomes us. We are never unworthy; he has made that abundantly clear in the supreme act of sacrifice that he made on our behalf.

PART THREE

coming alive
in prayer

imagine that!

I was at the Easter Vigil Mass with a friend who was coming into the Church that night. Our babysitting plans had fallen through, so I ended up going alone. On my way to the church, I was disappointed that I was all by myself. It wasn't until I was settled in my pew that I realized what a gift this was. I had several hours *alone*, something that is very rare in my life and, to top it off, I was at Mass. I found myself getting excited to have such an opportunity to pray, to listen and to reflect on my own with God.

I truly entered into the Mass. During the homily, I caught something that would last for months in my prayer. The priest started with a humorous image. He asked us to imagine the Gospel reading being acted out.

"What part would you want to play?" he asked us. "The guard? The angel? Jesus? I'd want to be the stone. After all, who else could just take it all in, with no lines to memorize?" We all laughed.

Yet the image struck me deeply. I imagined being the stone, just taking in this incredible miracle that would forever alter the course of history.

The priest continued. "Did you ever wonder why the stone was rolled away? Surely Jesus didn't need it to be moved to get out, so why was it rolled away? The stone was rolled away not so Jesus could come out but so that we could *go in*!"

Wow, that line hung with me for weeks. I kept contemplating the empty tomb, into which I had never even thought about going. The readings during the days after Easter lent themselves nicely to this journey: Every day there were stories about the disciples or Mary Magdalene visiting the tomb and going inside to find it empty.

The next time I went to see my spiritual director, I shared the whole experience. His first question was, what is happening with the image now? At that point it actually had stopped. He went on to ask me several other questions: "What was it like inside the tomb? Was it cold? What did it smell like? Did you hear any sounds? What was God trying to show you through it all?"

I didn't have any answers. The whole experience had been wonderful, but I really didn't penetrate it; I couldn't even tell you why I had experienced it. I realized that there was much more God wanted to do through this in my prayer. In my director's words, I needed to "milk" the image for all it was worth, continuing to spend time with it in my prayer until God was finished. I needed to engage all my senses—sight, hearing, touch, taste and smell.

So for the next several weeks, I kept returning to the tomb. I would envision myself sitting inside, trying to imagine what it would smell like, what the temperature would be and so on. At first it didn't seem as if much was happening. But after a week or so, the image started coming to life again. I got caught up in it; I wouldn't want to stop praying, even when I had to get to work.

This lasted almost till Pentecost that year. My experiences inside the empty tomb, some days more than others, were overall truly glorious tastes of the goodness of the Lord (see Psalm 34:8).

Toward the end of the Easter season, the image of the empty tomb transitioned into something different. At first I wasn't sure what it was; I just knew I was in a different place. I kept praying, trying to engage my spiritual senses deep within my heart and allow God to reveal this new location to me. It had a sweet smell, like flowers. It was warm and inviting. This place was immense; I couldn't seem to find the end of it.

Eventually God showed me that the place I was in now was the womb of Mary. For several days I kept receiving powerful Scripture passages about Mary, which led me to a much greater understanding of her role in my life and to a deeper relationship with her.

CHRISTIAN IMAGINATION

Everything we have been talking about—honesty, consistency, acknowledge, relate, receive, respond, a relationship and so on—*how* do we do it? These things we are talking about are spiritual realities. How do we access them?

I have talked with many young people over the years about prayer, and the most common thing I hear is, "I never hear God say anything to me." How do we talk with God when he is a spirit, and we are human? How do we hear him? And for that matter, how do we see or smell or taste anything in our prayer time? Doesn't it all sound a bit hokey?

Well, if you think it sounds a bit hokey, then you might need to take it up with God himself. The Scriptures are filled with references to seeing and hearing and tasting: "God saw that the light was good" (Genesis 1:4); They "have eyes to see, but see not, ... ears to hear, but hear not; for they are a rebellious house" (Ezekiel. 12:2); "This is why I speak to them in parables, because seeing they do not see, and hearing they do not hear, nor do they understand" (Matthew 13:13); "Taste and see that the LORD is good" (Psalm 34:8).

These passages seem to refer to something beyond the physical realm. In fact, they refer to a set of "spiritual senses"—spiritual counterparts to all of our physical senses. Yes, we are human, but we are also spirit, and our spiritual nature has senses just as our physical body does. We have an interior capacity, through the gift of Christian imagination, to access the spiritual realm through these spiritual senses. They allow us to seize spiritual realities and translate them so they are sensible to us. Christian imagination is a gift that allows us to be in contact with a part of reality that we can't be in contact with any other way.[1]

Saint Francis de Sales tells us: "[I]n use of simple imagination...we represent to ourselves the Savior in his sacred humanity as if he were near us, just as we sometime imagine a friend to be present."[2]

Authentic Christian imagination, while a great benefit in prayer, requires careful discernment. It is critical to distinguish between it and fantasy. Christian imagination allows us to seize upon spiritual realities that we otherwise would not be able to access. But these things are rooted in reality, whereas fantasy is not. This is one of the fundamental distinctions between imagination and fantasy.

A popular Catholic writer, Frank Sheed, actually criticizes human imagination. He states that since the fall of man, one of the results has been an out-of-hand imagination, which "plays a part in the mind's affairs totally out of proportion to its merits." Imagination, he says, can hinder the development of intellect. If one allows the imagination to be the guiding force for one's life, rather than the intellect, that can lead to trouble.[3]

I believe the word *fantasy* more accurately captures what Sheed is referring to here. Any imagination not guided by the intellect and by the reality of things is nothing more than fantasy. Christian imagination is an access point to spiritual realities in prayer, not a guiding force in life.

One of the hallmarks of Christian imagination in prayer is that *Jesus* is at the center. When anyone or anything other than Jesus is at the center of my attention, I have slipped away from Christian imagination and into fantasy.

In chapter three I identified different levels of the heart and clarified the fact that the Holy Spirit is not the only source moving at the deepest level. There also are the human spirit and the evil spirit. When we pray it is absolutely crucial to distinguish between the activity of these other sources and authentic movements from God.

If the activity or movement is not from God, then we need to reject it. This is a critical point, so I stress it. The enemy of our human nature, whether directly or through some manipulation of our human spirit, will constantly try to dislodge our prayer. Careful discernment is necessary, even in the midst of our prayer, to make sure that what we are receiving is truly from God.

Christian imagination, rooted in the reality of things and used with careful discernment, opens up a world of possibilities in prayer. It allows us to enter into the sacred Scriptures and place ourselves right there with whatever we are reading. We can walk on the road to Emmaus with the disciples. We can experience the Transfiguration with Peter, James and John. We can stand at the foot of the cross with John and Mary. We can go into the tomb and spend time there. We can be in the Upper Room at Pentecost.

Through this great gift of imagination, God invites us into a vibrant experience of prayer where we can engage all of our senses and all of our human faculties. It is a way that he can speak to us, reveal himself to us, reveal us to ourselves, direct us and draw us ever more deeply into the richness of his incredible love for us.

A DISCERNED PRAYER

I was talking with my twelve-year-old son one day as he was trying to work through some difficult circumstances. I felt as if the conversation was not really bearing any fruit. We seemed to be talking in circles, and he was getting increasingly frustrated.

I finally asked him if he would be willing to pray with me. At first I think he was annoyed, but he went along with it. I suggested he use Christian imagination to find himself in some place he had been that was really peaceful. He quickly picked a beautiful valley that he had visited a couple weeks earlier, when he was on a trip with his school. I had him describe the scene to me, asking questions that would cause him to engage his senses: sounds, smells, sights and so on.

Within a few minutes my son seemed to be completely absorbed with what he was imagining. His eyes were closed, and his face looked content. He described himself as sitting on a small ledge overlooking this beautiful valley. The ledge stuck out slightly from the ridge, giving the sense of "hanging" above the valley (his words). A gentle breeze was blowing; the sun was out, but it wasn't too hot.

As he engaged this scene with his imagination, I asked him to invite Jesus to come and sit with him on the ledge. He did this, and when it seemed that he had had enough time to adjust to this new image, I asked him to turn and look at Jesus, to look him in the eyes.

"Tell him what you are feeling in your heart," I said to him.

But very abruptly this incredibly peaceful experience turned into a disaster. My son started screaming and crying uncontrollably. It was so startling, I almost jumped out of my chair. I had him open his eyes, and I tried to find out what had happened. When he calmed down, he was able to tell me that when he looked at Jesus, Jesus put his hand on the back of his neck, pushed him off the ledge and said, "Go to hell, Aaron!"

I was stunned. How could this happen? Here I was trying to help my son pray through some very difficult circumstances. I had him enter into his heart and was leading him to relate to Jesus the deep feelings there, then *bam*, the whole thing went south on me!

I quickly realized that what was happening was the work of the enemy. So I told my son that Jesus would never say or do anything like that, and he needed to reject that thought right away. I led him in a simple yet decisive prayer of rejection, followed by a new prayer for receptivity. It was a bit challenging to return to the peaceful place we had been, but I knew it was critical to reclaim this whole experience for Jesus.

We finally got there, and I led Aaron to the same encounter with Jesus. He looked right into Jesus' eyes and told him of his struggles, *relating* what was going on his heart. There was a long time of silence, but I could tell that something was happening. He had tears running down his cheeks, yet he had a very peaceful look on his face. It finally ended, and he opened his eyes.

I asked him if he could share what had happened. He told me that he had shared everything with Jesus, and it felt good to just get everything off his chest. Then Jesus put his hands on either side of his face, looked right into his eyes and said, "Breathe." Aaron really didn't understand what that meant, but it made him really peaceful, as if everything was going to be OK. His whole demeanor had changed, all the agitation that I had been experiencing for the past hour was gone, all his anxiety over his troubling situation was gone.

Several times in the next couple weeks, my son thanked me for that experience. He said in particular that the image of Jesus gently putting his hands on either side of his face was one he kept going back to. It made him feel really good about himself.

What I have described here is a perfect example of all that we have been talking about. My son was deeply troubled, even experiencing some desolate thoughts and feelings—fundamentally spiritual ones at the deepest level of his heart. I tried to talk him through the situation but realized that I was just trying to fix it and figure it out for him. By the inspiration of the Holy Spirit, I was moved to lead him into prayer with all his troubles. I helped him *acknowledge* his deep thoughts and feelings. Then I helped him, through the gift of Christian imagination, *relate* those deep feelings to Jesus.

Remember, with Christian imagination, careful discernment is always necessary. Is this authentically from God or not? Aaron's first experience was clearly *not* from God, so we rejected it and persevered in prayer, even praying for greater receptivity. And what did my son receive? I will never know completely, but he clearly *received* peace that removed all the turmoil and anxiety he had been experiencing. I helped him *respond* in thanksgiving to the Lord for being with him in his prayer and for the beautiful image he had received.

In addition, my son's experience became what my spiritual director calls "an incarnational hook." The image he saw in prayer was one that he returned to over and over again during the next several days. Each time he did, it reconnected him to this deep feeling of peace and contentment.

You can see the critical importance of discerning what we receive in prayer making sure it is authentically from God. It is crucial to have a basic knowledge of your heart and to recognize the sources (the Holy Spirit, the human spirit and the evil spirit) of thoughts, feelings and desires, particularly in the deepest level of your heart.

I'm sure as my son matures, as he becomes more and more informed about who God is and how God relates to us, he won't be so quickly thrown by something that is so clearly *not* from God. As he has experiences in prayer that are authentically from God, he will become more familiar with God's voice and with subtle moves in his heart. He'll find counterfeit experiences much easier to identify and dismiss.

And that is exactly the type of maturity in prayer that this book is inviting us all into. It is an invitation to a new and constant awareness of the movement and work of God in our hearts, recognizing how he is trying to love us in the midst of our daily lives.

GOD'S TALKING

One final thought here: I find that many people struggle with whether something they experience in prayer is really from God. Their constant doubt causes them to all but abandon prayer.

I had an experience not long ago with my daughter, who is only ten. (Sorry for so many examples from my kids, but I figure if children can apply these principles, any young adult can as well!) She told me what I hear frequently from many young adults: "God never talks to me. I talk to him, but he never says anything back." Do you ever feel like that?

One day I decided to pray with her and see if I could help her. She had been struggling the previous several days with moodiness, even anger. She was constantly snapping at her brothers, losing her temper and so on.

I asked my daughter why she was angry and in turn encouraged her to ask Jesus if he would show her what was going on. I was trying to help her get in touch with the movements in her heart—the thoughts, feelings and desires. There wasn't a lot of clarity for her: She just knew that she was mad.

I led her in some simple prayers to help her focus on Jesus and clear her mind of distractions, and specifically for the grace of receptivity. Then I helped her *relate* her anger to Jesus, not trying to figure it all out but just giving it to him and asking *him* for clarity.

She was silent for a long time; I worried that she had fallen asleep on me. But she eventually opened her eyes and had a big smile on her face. I asked her what she had experienced. Had she heard God?

She quickly said, "No, I don't think so. But I feel different."

I asked her to share what she did experience. She told me that she had these thoughts go through her mind: (1) everything would be better when she finished her science fair project, (2) she needed to stop yelling at her brothers and (3) she was really beautiful.

I was amazed at this clarity of thought coming from a ten-year-old. I asked why she was smiling. She answered, "I just think it's funny that I thought I was beautiful."

I grabbed a piece of paper and drew a heart on it. I showed her that deep in her heart there were actually three different sources of the thoughts, feelings and desires that she could experience at any given moment: the Holy Spirit, her human spirit and the evil spirit. Then I went back and considered each of the three things she had "heard" in her mind and asked the question, "Where do you think this came from?"

The first thing she heard was probably from her human spirit, although it may have been influenced somewhat by the Holy Spirit. There was an aspect of revelation to the statement. Up until that point I don't believe she was aware why she was so agitated and angry. This moment of prayer brought some clarity to all that, helping her see how stressed she was with her science fair project, yet at the same time recognizing that it soon was going to be over.

The second thing she heard, about yelling at her brothers, was not from God; it was most likely from her. It was the voice of her conscience, letting her know that she was not being virtuous.

But that third statement had God's fingerprints all over it. It was informing and inspiring her identity. It expressed God's deep love for her and provided consolation, drawing her attention away from worldly concerns and anxieties to a deeper reality, namely, her inherent beauty in the eyes of God.

I spent the next several minutes explaining all of this to her, especially how that third statement was not just a thought in her mind but was actually God talking to her: That's what his voice sounds like. She said, "But it sounds so much like my voice." How precious. I was simply helping my daughter to "hear" God, to know what it is was like to have him talk to you.

Later that night at the dinner table, we were going around the table sharing our highs and lows of the day. What a gift it was to hear my daughter say, "I heard God today. He talked to me and told me I was beautiful."

By the way, if you have any doubts about whether or not God speaks to you, let's put those to rest right now. He *does*! You may not be aware of it or recognize it, but he is communicating with you all the time. He speaks to you through the Scriptures, through nature, through your daily experiences and through other people. In fact, he dwells in your heart, a Trinity of Father, Son and Holy Spirit, laboring to love you in every moment, through all of creation. And in that labor he will often use your imagination to connect with you intimately and to communicate his loving plan directly to your heart.

make it a habit

One thing I remember from my childhood in northwest Iowa is the winter storms. They started with small flakes of snow blowing across our driveway. I would often watch out the window, wondering how much snow we would get, wondering most of all if school would be cancelled. Often the snow wouldn't amount to much at first, but if it was still coming down as I was going to bed, there was hope.

I would wake up in the morning and run to the window to see how much snow had fallen. But I wouldn't be able to see anything. The window would be covered!

Bountiful snow was not uncommon where I grew up. We also had the wind, which would blow the snow into huge drifts. I remember high walls of snow, higher than our car, bordering the roads all winter long.

And it would all start with little flakes.

Another story I heard once makes the same point I want to make with my snow story. I picked it up at a training seminar, and there was no author credited.

> I am your constant companion. I will push you forward to success, or I will drag you down to failure. I am completely at your command. Eighty percent of what you do, you might as well hand over to me, and I will do it promptly, and I will do it correctly. I am easily managed; you must merely be firm with me. Show me what you'd like to have done, and after a couple of lessons, I will do it automatically. I am the

servant of all great people. I am the servant of all failures as well.

Those who are great, I have made great. Those who are failures, I have made failures. I am not a machine, though I work with the precision of a machine and the intellect of a human. Take me, train me, be firm with me, and I'll place the world at your feet. Be easy with me, and I will destroy you! Who am I?

Who am I? I am your habits! And your habits, just like those snowflakes, have the power to become a formidable force in your life, for good or for ill. All great people were made great by the simple little daily decisions they consistently made. And all holy people were made holy by their ruthless commitment to consistent and honest relational prayer. There was no way they could make themselves holy; only God can do that. But the part that they could contribute—showing up and spending time with him and then being real and honest when they were there—they made a daily habit of in their lives.

DAY BY DAY

A number of years ago I found myself in the middle of absolute chaos. Two teens in our community decided to show up at school one day and start shooting their friends. *Columbine* has become a household word in our country. Three of the funerals were at our parish. Many students and parents are still struggling with the effects of that event.

One young woman asked me a good question: "How could anyone become so evil?" She was in the school that day, she lost dear friends, and she continues to struggle with why she didn't die too. Coming from her, the question is significant: She *saw* the evil firsthand.

I thought and thought about how to answer her. But in the end the answer was very simple. It's easy to become evil; it happens one simple choice at a time. Those little choices, made consistently over a long time, become a "mountain."

In the weeks and months after the shootings, I had opportunities to share this insight with our parish community. It became a message of hope in the midst of tragedy for us all. Because if you could become absolute, pure evil simply by making small, simple choices for evil consistently over time, then the opposite had to be true as well. If you made simple little choices for good, for love, for God, consistently over time, you would become holy, a saint.

Little things done consistently become a formidable force in our lives. The issue is which direction these habits are moving us. Saint Ignatius, in his rules for discernment, talks about "two *fundamental directions* of the spiritual life, as evidenced in Augustine's experience...: the *first* consists in movement *away from God* and *toward serious sin*; the *second*, the reverse of the first, consists in movement *toward God* and *away from serious sin*, indeed away from every form of sin, serious or otherwise."[1] Our habits often are the key to the direction in our life.

What are your spiritual habits?

I find that many young adults whom I talk with and mentor can't really articulate what their habits are. They have a loose system of things they do, depending on the week and how they feel on any particular day. I'm sorry, but that kind of system won't work if your true desire is to grow spiritually. If you want to build muscle mass or train for a race or triathlon, you can't approach it in a loosey-goosey way. The same is true of your spiritual life. If your desire is to grow, then you need a plan.

This is not a plan to do it ourselves. Always remember that only God can do the changing; only God can transform us. But our plan must involve the regular discipline of drawing ourselves near to God so he can do that work in us: daily prayer, regular reception of the sacraments, periodic extended times of prayer, occasional retreats and so on.

What's your plan for the next six months? For the next year?

I find that if I don't have a plan, and if I don't have other people who know what the plan is and hold me accountable to it, things tends to go the way of Rule 1—from bad to worse. My lack of discipline leads me away from the regular habit of daily prayer, then into a certain self-inflicted desolation, then to moments of temptation, eventually succumbing to those temptations and falling into sin. The whole process can take months, or a week, to develop.

But I usually find myself wondering how the heck I ended up in this place again. With reflection it's not too hard to see. It all started with a whimsical attitude toward the daily "habits" of my spiritual life. The words "Be easy with me, and I will destroy you" ring in my ears.

Psychological research has established twenty-one days as a sort of magical number when it comes to habits. It seems that if you can do something consistently for twenty-one days, you can make it a habit. This research is touted in all the self-help books on how to change your diet or your financial situation or your life.

I am *not* advocating trying to change yourself or even improve yourself (let God do that), but I am making a case for you to pray every day. If you're not in a habit of daily prayer right now, it may seem a bit overwhelming to make a commitment to this for the rest of your life. So could you make a commitment to pray every day for the next twenty-one days? My guess is that during that time you will begin experiencing the relationship Jesus offers you. After twenty-one days you will not continue just because you have formed a new habit but because you are falling in love with Jesus!

APPROACHES TO PRAYER

As you make a commitment to spending time in prayer, you need to have a concrete plan. I recommend you start with thirty minutes a day. You also want to think about what you are going to do with your time.

In his *Introduction to the Devout Life*, Saint Francis de Sales offers some practical advice on starting this prayer time. He specifically emphasizes the practice of "mental prayer, the prayer of the heart."[2] We have talked about this kind of prayer throughout this book.

Francis offers a simple method of preparation and then meditation. For the first part, preparation he gives two points: "(1) place yourself in the presence of God, and (2) invoke his assistance." He goes on to explain four principal means of placing oneself in the presence of God:

> The first consists of a lively, attentive realization of God's absolute presence, that is, that God is in all things and all places.
>
> The second...is to remember that he is not only in the place where you are but also that he is present in a most particular manner in your heart and in the very center of your spirit....
>
> A third way is to consider how our Savior in his humanity gazes down from heaven on all mankind and particularly on Christians, who are his children, and most especially on those who are at prayer....
>
> A fourth method consists in use of simple imagination when we represent to ourselves the Savior in his sacred humanity as if he were near us, just as we sometimes imagine a friend to be present.
>
> ...[Y]ou will employ one of these four means of placing yourself in the presence of God before prayer. Do not use them all at once, but only one at a time and that briefly and simply.[3]

The second aspect of the preparation for Saint Francis de Sales is the invocation. "[Y]our soul prostrates itself before him with the most profound reverence. It acknowledges that it is most unworthy to appear before such sovereign Majesty, but since it knows that this same supreme goodness wills that it should be so, it implores his grace in order to serve and adore him properly in this meditation."[4]

He also encourages calling on the assistance of your guardian angel and the saints in your prayer. "For example, when meditating on the death of our Lord, you can invoke our Lady, St. John, Mary Magdalen, and the good thief, begging that the affections and interior movements they then conceived may be shared with you."[5]

Saint Francis adds a third point to the preparation when we are meditating on a mystery of the faith: "This is simply to picture in imagination the entire mystery you wish to meditate on as if it really took place here before us. For example, if you wish to meditate on our Lord on the Cross, imagine that you are on Mount Calvary and that there you see and hear all that was done or said on the day of his passion."[6]

Then Saint Francis explains what he calls the second part of prayer, meditation. He refers to this as the follow-up to the work of the imagination, the "act of the intellect":

> This is simply to make one or more considerations in order to raise our affections to God and the things of God....
>
> [This] produces devout movements in the will, such as love of God and neighbor, desire for heaven and glory, zeal for the salvation of souls, imitation of the life of our Lord, compassion, awe, joy, fear of God's displeasure....
>
> However, you must not dwell so long on these general reflections...as to change them into special

and particular resolutions for your own correction and improvement.[7]

And finally Saint Francis talks about the conclusion to prayer:

> [We] must conclude our meditation with three acts.... The first is the act of thanksgiving, by which we return thanks to God for the affections and resolutions he has given us and for his goodness and mercy.... The second is the act of offering, by which we offer to God his own goodness and mercy, his Son's death, Blood, and virtues, and in union with them our own affections and resolutions. The third act is that of supplication, by which we beseech God and implore him to share with us the graces and virtues of his Son and to bless our affections and resolutions so that we may faithfully fulfill them.[8]

In these few pages of *Introduction to the Devout Life*, Saint Francis lays out a very simple plan for a daily prayer time. You can see the essential dynamics of prayer that we have talked about in this book clearly evident in this method. First, you prepare your heart (*acknowledge*), then meditate on some mystery of the faith, which leads to certain affections, to which you open yourself as much as you can and then relate back to God (*relate and receive*). This new affection leads to a natural resolution, inspired by what you have just received from God (*respond*). The conclusion expresses that natural response, and inherent in the whole method is the element of relationship.

SOME REAL-LIFE PRAYERS

As clear as Saint Francis' outline is, every relationship with Jesus is going to take on a different look and feel, simply because every person has a unique personality. Jesus has the ability to relate to each and every one of us just as we are.

I thought it would be helpful to share here several different approaches to prayer by young adults. Each example has the essential elements present, but each according to the unique personality of the person praying.

Andy

Over the years since my conversion, it has become more and more necessary to have a long period of time in my daily prayer that is set aside for simply being with Jesus. It helps me "detox," unwind and settle into the peace that is present in my heart. I often am silent this way for most of the hour.

I also use spiritual reading as a springboard for conversation with God. I have found that the Liturgy of the Hours is an amazing way to keep prayer grounded in both Scripture (especially the psalms) and conversation. I also have a huge devotion to Saint Thérèse of Lisieux. We have a similar outlook on the Lord and life, so I often spend time with her writings when it bears fruit.

Another staple of my prayer life is journaling. Maybe it is because I am so easily distracted or because so much of my life is necessarily "noisy," but I often find that writing down my prayer to the Lord helps me focus, and it allows me to express the thoughts and desires of my heart that are sometimes hard to express.

Kristina

I usually try to set aside a sufficient amount of time, at least thirty minutes, to pray before I go to bed. I always take a minute or two to ask the Holy Spirit to come. I then do an examination of conscience.

Sometimes if there isn't something pressing on my heart that I need to talk to Jesus about, I do Night Prayer. From there I usually tell the Lord about my day, good things and bad things that have happened. Usually there is one thought or feeling that occurred throughout the day, sometimes more than one, and I ask the Lord to help me see why I felt that particular way or what he is saying to me through those thoughts or feelings. Usually this leads me to journal, which helps me see and hear things more clearly.

The rest of the prayer time I spend in silence, listening to Christ. Sometimes he says things to me, and sometimes he just lets me rest in silence.

Jonathan

I like to pray for thirty minutes to an hour each day. My prayer usually has a similar structure, but the details may vary.

Most days I begin by reading a psalm as a way to praise God for who he is. I like using the psalms for this because I believe that they praise God in more beautiful words than I could ever use. After reading a psalm I may meditate on the words for a bit. I proceed to thank God for my day and for all the ways in which he has blessed me.

Then I might read a passage of Scripture, sometimes a random passage and sometimes one previously picked out, like the Mass readings for that day. Sometimes I pray a rosary or simply meditate. When I meditate I quiet my heart and pray for the grace to remain receptive to God. After that I pray for other people.

I end my time with this simple prayer: "Lord, be on my mind, be on my lips, and be in my heart, that I may know thy word, speak thy word and become thy word."

Meg

As a mother of five, I have learned from experience that I can't just "pray"; I have to set up my prayer time and try to anticipate what *distractions* may come up in those thirty to forty-five minutes. When I don't do this, there are numerous interruptions, which are quickly followed by desolate thoughts of abandoning my prayer altogether. I have had some success in setting up my prayer during our baby's naps, with my older kids helping me by watching the younger ones.

I practice the daily examen (see section below) before I go to bed, so I usually begin my morning prayer time by drawing myself into God's presence and then recalling the most predominant thought, feeling or desire, whether consoling or desolate, from my examen the evening before. I typically have a plan for my prayer time—reading Scripture, praying the rosary or the Liturgy of the Hours and so on. But as I am implementing that plan, my focus is on relating that predominant thought, feeling or desire to the Lord.

If while I am reading or praying, something grabs my attention, I stop and try to listen. How does God want to love me, inform my identity, inspire me, heal me or reveal himself to me? I try to be as receptive as I can to how God is loving me throughout my prayer, even praying that God would help me receive!

Finally, I spend time reflecting on what my resolution for the day should be. How did God love me today in prayer? How do I need to respond to that love? I close by acknowledging each person of the Trinity and the Blessed Mother, especially for their presence to me during the prayer time.

THE DAILY EXAMEN

Another spiritual tool Saint Ignatius gives us is the daily examen prayer. Not to be confused with an examination of conscience, though some elements of the examen prayer encompass a review of thoughts and actions of the day, the examen is "a *way of praying* that opens our eyes to God's daily self-revelation and increasingly clarifies for us our own responses to it."[9] I have found incredible simplicity yet rich power in this way of praying. I offer it here as an additional spiritual discipline for you to consider making one of your daily habits in prayer.

The examen prayer can be outlined as follows:

Transition. Begin by relaxing into God's presence. Become aware of the love with which God looks upon you.

Gratitude. Focus on the concrete, uniquely personal gift you've been blessed with, whether obviously important or apparently insignificant, with a deep realization that *all is gift.* Note the gifts that God's love has given you this day, and give thanks to God for them.

Prayer for light. Ask God for insight and strength to make this examen a work of grace, fruitful beyond your own human capacity. Ask for the light to know yourself as the Holy Spirit knows you.

Review. Look at the day with God. Look for the stirrings in your heart and the thoughts that God has given you this day. Also look for those that have not been from God. Review your choices in response to both and throughout the day in general.

It is also helpful to choose an experience from the day that seems to be the most significant or dominant and reflect on that experience with the following questions:

1. Where was God in this experience?
2. Was I receptive to him and his love in this situation?
3. In what area of my heart is God especially calling for conversion through this experience?

Sorrow and contrition. Repent for not responding to what the Lord asked of you today. This sorrow is a hopeful and "awe-ful" recognition of your inability to respond wholeheartedly to the Lord and, at the same time, of your trust in his faithful and personal love for you. Ask for the healing touch of the forgiving God, who with love and respect for you removes your heart's burdens.

Renewal. Look to the following day and, with God, plan concretely how to live it in accord with his loving desire for your life. With a faith-filled vision and a discerning mind and heart, stand before the Lord with a desire to see him in all things. Your hope for the immediate future will be expressed uniquely and in petition each time you pray the examen.[10]

LECTIO DIVINA

Another prayer method that has been a rich part of Catholic spirituality is *lectio divina*. Pope Benedict XVI has mentioned it specifically many times: "My dear young friends, I urge you to become familiar with the Bible, and to have it at hand so it can be your compass pointing out the road to follow. By reading it, you will learn to know Christ.... A time-honoured way to study and savor the Word of God is *lectio divina* which constitutes a real and veritable *spiritual journey* marked out in stages."[11] And in another address: "[T]his practice will bring the Church—I am convinced of it—a new spiritual springtime."[12]

This method of prayer involves a slow, contemplative "praying" of the Scriptures, which allows the Bible, the Word of God, to become a means of union with God. Of all the methods of prayer, *lectio divina* is one that most clearly exemplifies the essential dynamics of prayer that we have talked about in this book. I have taken the elements of *lectio* and showed how they are a unique expression of each essential dynamic of prayer.

These first four steps are preparation for *lectio divina*:

Place and time. It helps to have a consistent and quiet place and time for prayer.

Posture. Be relaxed and comfortable but not in a posture conducive to sleep.

Passage. Choose a passage from Scripture.

Pray. Ask the Holy Spirit to lead your prayer. The Holy Spirit is the teacher of your prayer.

Allow these final four steps to weave in and out of your time of meditation. Let the Holy Spirit, the teacher of your prayer, lead you.

> *Lectio.* Prayerfully read the Scripture passage you have chosen. Pause when you feel yourself drawn to a word, phrase or thought.
>
> *Meditatio (acknowledge).* Ponder this passage and what it means for you. Use your imagination, and engage your spiritual senses! Pay attention to and acknowledge the thoughts, feelings and desires that accompany the detail that has arrested your attention.
>
> *Oratio (relate).* Talk with God about the passage and your reflection. Honestly relate to the Father, Son and Holy Spirit what has come up in your heart.
>
> *Contemplatio (receive).* When God so moves, rest in his quiet presence, and surrender to grace. When ready, return to your reading.[13]

WHAT WORKS FOR YOU?

There are many other ways to pray. There's the Liturgy of the Hours, the rosary, praise and worship and quiet meditation, to mention just a few. The richness and beauty of Catholic spirituality has so much to offer that you could never capture it all.

The important thing is to find what works for you. This is about *your* relationship, and *you* are going to have a unique way of connecting with God in prayer. And don't be surprised when what works for you now doesn't work for you later. As your relationship with Jesus grows, and you change, your experience of prayer is going to change as well.

CHAPTER NINE
the journey

Many spiritual writers refer to the spiritual life as a journey. The *Catechism of the Catholic Church*, in its very first paragraph, defines this journey:

> God, infinitely perfect and blessed in himself, in a plan of sheer goodness freely created man to make him share in his own blessed life. For this reason, at every time and in every place, God draws close to man. He calls man to seek him, to know him, to love him with all his strength. He calls together all men, scattered and divided by sin, into the unity of his family, the Church. To accomplish this, when the fullness of time had come, God sent his Son as Redeemer and Savior. In his Son and through him, he invites men to become, in the Holy Spirit, his adopted children and thus heirs of his blessed life. (*CCC*, 1)

One of my professors rearticulated this paragraph in these words: "the journey from blessing to blessing." Our very origin comes from the blessedness of God, and our end, our ultimate goal, is to return to that very same blessed life. Because we know where we come from and where we're going, we also have a purpose. And there *is* a plan for this in our lives, "a plan of sheer goodness" designed by God himself. These are welcome words in our culture and times, in a world that seems lacking and confused on these points.

At the very heart of this journey—in fact, the means to the journey itself—is a life of prayer. This spiritual journey is what is *real*.

But live long enough on the "outside" of yourself, and you will be tempted to believe that all the temporary things of this world are what is real and that the spiritual life is somehow a figment of your imagination. It's funny how it works. The very thing that *is* reality we dismiss as fantasy, all the while clinging to a fantasy under some delusion that *it* is reality. Don't let yourself be deluded! As Pope Saint Leo the Great said, "Rouse yourself, man, and recognize the dignity of your nature. Remember that you were made in God's image; though corrupted in Adam, that image has been restored in Christ."[1]

We were made for a purpose, a holy purpose. And what we do with the time we have, the *role* we play in the story, is crucial. So play your part well!

THE FACE OF REALITY

This fundamental confusion about the reality of things is a stumbling block for many. Prayer is one of the ways that God will define reality for us. The more time we spend with him, the more we will begin to understand the face of reality and see reality the way he sees it—and the way the Church sees it, for she sees it as he does. So in addition to prayer, we must allow ourselves to be formed by what God has taught us about reality through the Church.

First of all, there is no way to see reality the way God does without knowing the story of how he has worked and revealed himself throughout history. Frank Sheed wrote: "[Man's] relation to God has a history, a shape, an unfolding; in fact, a plot.... Not to know the story is not to know the religion; and not to know the religion is not to know reality."[2] (I'm borrowing a lot from Frank Sheed in this chapter; his book *Theology and Sanity* has some great wisdom.)

Second, reality cannot be seen unless it is seen in its fullness. The problem is, we tend to want to break things up into parts. With reality this cannot be done.

> Nothing is rightly seen save in the totality to which it belongs; no part of the Universe is rightly seen save in relation to the whole. But the Universe cannot be seen as a whole unless one sees God as the Source of existence of every part of it and the center by relation to which every part is related to every other.... Just as knowing that all things are upheld by God is a first step in knowing *what* we are, so a clear view of the shape of reality is a first step toward knowing *where* we are. To know where we are and what we are—that would seem to be the very minimum required by our dignity as human beings.[3]

Rouse yourself, man!

And what is the reality of things, the way God sees it, the way the Church sees it? It's not a great mystery that the leaders of our Church keep hidden; it's right out there for all of us to grasp, to study. In fact, because of modern technology, it's more accessible today than it was for any other generation in the history of the Church.

Sheed offers an outline of the real universe, "the face of reality: God, infinite and eternal, Trinity, Unity; humanity, finite, created in time, fallen and redeemed by Christ; the individual human person born into the life of nature, reborn into the life of grace, united with Christ in the Church which is His Mystical Body, aided by angels, hindered by devils, destined for heaven, in peril of hell."[4] There it is in a nutshell—who God is, who we are, how we got here, where we fit into the universe and the challenges we face.

We are destined for heaven, but that's not all: We have not been left to ourselves to get there. In fact, on our own we don't stand a chance. But *God* is sufficient; he has provided *all* that is necessary. The "work" of our lives, the task before us here on earth, is simple: to avail ourselves of what he provides.

In the sacrament of baptism, we are reborn to the life of grace. We are given a new life-principle.

> Though...meant primarily to enable [man] to live in heaven, [this new life] is given...while he is still upon earth, and its acquisition and preservation are man's principal business on earth.... It is not a gift given once for all. It may be lost and restored. What is more vital, it may be increased. While we live, there is no limit to the possibility of the growth of this life in us.... [T]here is no limit to the increase of its energizing in us, save the limit of our willingness to lay ourselves open to it.[5]

In his plan of sheer goodness, God ordained that the Church and the sacraments would be the vehicle to get this life into us.

But the reality is that this new life comes into a nature that is broken: "we have this treasure in earthen vessels" (2 Corinthians 4:7).

> [G]race does not supply us with a new nature but works in the nature it finds.... Grace is necessary for the healing of our nature. But it will not itself heal our nature. Our cooperation with grace will do that, and in the measure of our cooperation. We are the trouble....
>
> ...Grace gives us a power to act supernaturally.... But though it gives us the power to act supernaturally, it does not remove our power to act sinfully. It does not even remove our natural desire to act sinfully. What it does is to insert a new desire to act for the love of God, so that there is a new war in our powers....
>
> Thus our problem is to bring our natural habits into harmony with our supernatural habits.[6]

Our supernatural habits may deeply desire time with God in prayer, while our natural habits would desire more time in bed! "Grace has to operate through our faculties; we have to work for the destruction of habits that make our faculties bad instruments and for the development of habits that will make them good instruments—to the point where the supernature has become a sort of second nature."[7]

This is what we would call the formation of virtue. Our part is to cooperate with grace, to labor to grow virtue by "the steady repetition of actions, actions against the bad habit, actions tending to form a good habit."[8] Get out of bed to pray more times than you decide to sleep, and eventually a new habit will be formed. But get some resolve about you. This way of living isn't easy, nor should it be.

For most of us physical exercise doesn't come naturally. If you want to stay in shape, you have to decide to overcome your natural inclinations to "rest easy." Oh, how I wish it came naturally. It's *hard* work: first overcoming our avoidance of discomfort and then pushing ourselves to ever-increasing levels of strain. Yet those who excel overcome all this. They conquer themselves before they ever conquer the athletic feat they are pursuing.

Neither does the interior life come naturally. Why is it that so many people can push through seemingly endless obstacles to work out, but when *one* hurdle presents itself to prayer or spiritual disciplines, most seem to falter? I believe that if we are going to succeed in the spiritual journey, we need to approach our spirituality a bit more like our workout schedule.

ACCESSING GRACE

This is our part: to cooperate with grace, to invite more of it into our lives by disposing ourselves to what is available: Mass and the sacraments, the Word of God, community with other believers, prayer.

> [I]f the body must be brought into right relation with the mind, the mind must be brought into right relation with God. And the obvious method is prayer. Prayer does of itself, even more directly than suffering, tend to correct the disharmony between ourselves and reality.... [I]t brings the soul into that sort of contact with God in which He is closest and clearest.[9]

But what happens when no one else sees reality the way we have described it here? How do we live this way when everyone around us seems to be going another direction? As the young adult I shared about earlier asked, "How can God be real when so many people don't even believe in him?" It is difficult to remain faithful when it seems as if everyone around you has abandoned faith altogether.

First, remember that the spiritual life is a journey, which implies a direction. There *is* a destination and, as we said in chapter five, we're either moving toward that destination or moving away from it. There's no standing still or parking. If everyone else seems to be going in a different direction, know that it's the *wrong* direction.

But more importantly, I would say that without a ruthless commitment to regular prayer, it will be impossible to go against the tide. When we pray regularly, we become increasingly aware of God's pursuit of *us*. Our commitment to consistency and honesty are rewarded with God's hope and love, his presence and his promise. A praying life is not just helpful; it's truly living! Father Pedro Arrupe, the late father general of the Jesuits, said:

> Nothing is more practical than finding God, that is, than falling in love in a quite absolute, final way. What you are in love with, what seizes your imagination, will affect everything. It will decide what will get you out of bed in the morning, what you will do with your

evenings, how you will spend your weekends, what
you read, who you know, what breaks your heart, and
what amazes you with joy and gratitude. Fall in love,
stay in love, and it will decide everything.[10]

It is in our prayer that God can console us in our feelings of alone-
ness, that God can inform and inspire who we are and why we are
here. It's in prayer that he will remind us of his incredible love for
us. It's in prayer that he will inspire us with the conviction to stay
strong, to keep up the good fight.

It's in a life of prayer that God will remind us that we are not
alone, and in fact there are countless stories of those who have
gone before us who have stayed the course no matter the cost. In
prayer Jesus will draw us into the story for ourselves, allowing us
to participate in such grand events as his baptism in the Jordan,
the Transfiguration, the agony in the garden and his crucifixion.
There is no end to the mysteries we can share in. Prayer is an
adventure, and a grand one at that!

We don't have to do a lot to keep moving forward in this
journey, but we need to do something. We've got to keep moving
forward—no matter how insignificant our progress may seem!
Remember those little, seemingly insignificant snowflakes, falling
consistently over time, that combine to make a formidable force.

THE ADVENTURE OF THE INTERIOR LIFE

Some of my favorite movies are *The Lord of the Rings* trilogy—I
love all three of them. The years that they came to the theaters, I
bought large groups of tickets, trying to get anyone I could to go
see them. By the time *Return of the King* came out, the third install-
ment, I think we came close to buying out half of the theater!

What I love so much about these stories is how they convey
the "journey." The story of Frodo and the ring seems to have many

similarities to the overall story of salvation, and so much of it is like our own lives. I like to show clips from these films to illustrate points when I'm talking to groups.

We are all on a journey not unlike the journey that Frodo was on. There are going to be lots of hardships and challenges; there also will be times of great joy. We will find a few people who will travel with us, yet sometimes we will find ourselves feeling very alone. And just when we think we can go no further, someone like Gandalf, Sam or Aragorn will show up and help carry us along. The story inspires us to believe that we too can reach our goal.

But there's another interpretation of the story that I have discovered in the past year. The story isn't just an analogy about our journey in the world; we can also look at it as an analogy of an *interior* journey.

We all have landscapes in our hearts like those in the story: the Shire, Rohan, Rivendell, Isengard, Minas Tirith, Moria, Mordor—places that are filled with peace and joy and others that are filled with desolation, depression and evil. From day to day we can find ourselves in one landscape or another because of the movements in our heart. We'd like to stay in places like the Shire and Rivendell, almost pretending that Mordor doesn't exist, but at times Mordor does spring up in us, and we must address what is there.

The point is that the journey of our hearts toward God is an exciting adventure. It is a journey that Jesus is inviting us on. He desires to lead us on this adventure to reclaim every area of our heart, to defeat the evil within us and drive it completely away.

Some battles are going to be decisive ones, like the battle with the Balrog in the mines of Moria and the battles at Helm's Deep and Minas Tirith. These decisive victories will bring freedom that we have never known before, and with each one we will experience greater depth in our relationship with God, because it will give him more "room" in our heart.

Ultimately that is the whole point of the journey. God desires to get his very life inside us. That life, because of God's nature, is expansive, life-generating, all-encompassing. We can't contain his life to a certain area of our life or heart: He wants it throughout. And our life on this earth is the chance we have to grow our capacity for that life.

"Whatever capacity the soul has grown to at death, that capacity will be filled in the glory and the joy of heaven."[11] Our chance to overcome ourselves, our chance to become more and more love to others, our pursuit of God's life—it all comes to an end at the moment of our death. And the capacity that we have allowed ourselves to be expanded to by the work of the Trinity is the level to which we will be filled with God in heaven.

To expand our capacity for God in this life is going to require more than the status quo. Settling for a mediocre life of prayer, for inconsistency and downright laziness in our pursuit of virtue, for complacency because we actually think we're "doing pretty good compared to everyone around us"—this type of attitude is *not* going to get us to our goal.

But in a life of regular prayer, God will gradually and in stages draw us more deeply into the mystery of himself. And with every increasing level of depth, we will have less and less desire for ourselves or anything else that distracts us from him. The pursuit of holiness will be less toil, less beating ourselves into submission and more falling in love.

I can't tell you the number of things that have fallen away from my life since I met my wife. It hasn't been a huge burden either. I didn't have to extract those things from my life; they sort of fell away because I lost interest.

I know that some battles will require personal hardship for full surrender. But I do believe that for the most part, if we are praying consistently and honestly in a relationship of prayer with the Trinity, the desire of love will eventually far outweigh the desire for anything else.

WHY IT'S ALL WORTH IT

In the end will it all be worth it? Living this life, possibly in the midst of ridicule and persecution—will it really be worth it? The answer is simple. *Yes! Yes! Yes!* There is not a doubt in my mind!

Now, there are doubts frequently in my heart, sometimes overwhelming doubts that cause me to waver in conviction, even falter in my steps. But being aware of those movements in my heart and having a relationship with the one to whom I can relate them makes all the difference in the world. When I honestly can relate them to God in prayer and relate them to other believers, especially those who understand the ways the enemy would try to use such doubts, I can return to what I know in my *mind* to be true, what God has revealed to be true and what the Church has told me I can have faith in through *reason* (see *CCC*, 50).

It's all worth it, because in the end I am promised full blessing. Remember, the goal of it all is heaven, "from blessing to blessing," and I'm convinced enough to know that in the end that's the one place I want to be. I don't want to *just* make it; I want to be as close to the action as I can be.

That's not just some prideful desire; it's birthed of a knowledge that whatever capacity for God I can receive in this life will make *this* life much more fulfilling. The more I am receptive to the life and love that God the Father, Son and Holy Spirit is offering me, the more my capacity for that life is expanded within me. Heaven is not just for the afterlife; we can have tastes of it here, even now.

Each one of us shares in Christ's identity and mission as priest, prophet and king. It is through the gift of relational prayer that we come to a fuller revelation of what that identity and mission really are and how to uniquely express them in our life. But

from a broad perspective, the Church already helps us understand
what these roles look like:

> On entering the People of God through faith and
> Baptism, one receives a share in this people's
> unique, *priestly* vocation.... "The baptized, by
> regeneration and the anointing of the Holy Spirit,
> are *consecrated* to be a spiritual house and a holy
> priesthood." (*CCC,* 784, quoting *Lumen Gentium,*
> 10; see Hebrews 5:1–5; Revelation 1:6)
>
> "The holy People of God shares also in Christ's
> *prophetic* office" ... when it "unfailingly adheres to
> this faith" ... and when it deepens its understand-
> ing and becomes Christ's witness in the midst of
> this world. (*CCC,* 785, quoting *Lumen Gentium,* 12;
> see Jude 3)
>
> Finally, the People of God shares in the *royal*
> office of Christ.... For the Christian, "to reign is to
> serve him," particularly when serving "the poor
> and the suffering, in whom the Church recognizes
> the image of her poor and suffering founder." ...
>
> ..."What, indeed, is as royal for a soul as to
> govern the body in obedience to God? And what is
> as priestly as to dedicate a pure conscience to the
> Lord and to offer the spotless offerings of devotion
> on the altar of the heart?" (*CCC,* 786, quoting
> *Lumen Gentium,* 8, see 36; St. Leo the Great,
> Sermon 4, 1: *Patrologia Latina* 54, 149)

Every time we take time to pray and "offer...devotion on the altar
of the heart," we share in the priestly office of Christ. Every time
we adhere to the faith and become a bold witness for Christ to the
world around us, we share in the prophetic office. And when we

reign over our own bodies, over our own passions and over our selfishness in order to make of ourselves a free, total, faithful and life-giving gift to others, we share in the royalty of Christ himself.

Imagine what that looks like, to live as a priest, prophet and king in this world today. It looks like total freedom! Imagine the Church like this! We wouldn't have enough room in our churches. If you want to live this way, to live with this kind of freedom, take time to pray, every day!

This foundational and core identity—priest, prophet and king—is already yours: It's *who* you are. In a life of relational prayer, with the assistance of the Church and Mary, this humanity of yours will be "knitted" into existence (see Psalm 139:13).

> "The Holy Spirit will come upon you, and the power of the Most High will overshadow you." (Lk. 1:35)
>
> May all of us wholeheartedly say with Mary, in all simplicity, humility and trust: "May it be done to me according to your word." (Lk. 1:38)[12]

testimonies

We take this journey with many others. It's good at times to hear how they are faring. In this closing chapter I have collected some stories that will inspire. Some are from saints who have already been named, others are from saints who are still on the journey of becoming. May these stories inspire you, as they have me, to keep pursuing God. There is no situation that you cannot relate to God and there find his constant labor of love as the sustaining force for your life!

A CLOUD OF WITNESSES

Let's start by looking at some words of wisdom from the saints in glory.

> I am certain that they refuse [to turn to God] because they imagine this kindly disposed God to be harsh and severe, this merciful God to be callous and inflexible, this lovable God to be cruel and oppressive…. What are you afraid of, you men of little faith? That he will not pardon your sins? But with his own hands he has nailed them to the cross. That you are used to soft living and your tastes are fastidious? But he is aware of our weakness. That a prolonged habit of sinning binds you like a chain? But the Lord loosens the shackles of prisoners. Or perhaps angered by the enormity and frequency of your sins he is slow to extend a helping hand? But where sin abounded, grace became superabundant.[1]
>
> —Saint Bernard of Clairvaux

It is my belief that to a person so disposed, God will not refuse that most intimate kiss of all, a mystery of supreme generosity and ineffable sweetness.[2]

—Saint Bernard of Clairvaux

O Jesus! why can't I tell all *little souls* how unspeakable is Your condescension? I feel that if You found a soul weaker and littler than mine, which is impossible, You would be pleased to grant it still greater favors, provided it abandoned itself with total confidence to Your Infinite Mercy. But why do I desire to communicate Your secrets of Love, O Jesus, for was it not You alone who taught them to me, and can You not reveal them to others? Yes, I know it, and I beg You to do it. I beg You to cast Your Divine Glance upon a great number of *little* souls. I beg You to choose a legion of *little* Victims worthy of Your LOVE![3]

—Saint Thérèse of Lisieux

O souls, created for these grandeurs and called to them! What are you doing? How are you spending your time? Your aims are base and your possessions miseries! O wretched blindness of your eyes! You are blind to so brilliant a light and deaf to such loud voices because you fail to discern that insofar as you seek eminence and glory you remain miserable, base, ignorant, and unworthy of so many blessings![4]

—Saint John of the Cross

A SOLDIER

As a first lieutenant in the United States Army, currently deployed in Iraq, I find myself in a desert, both physically and in my prayer life. I would like to share my recent experiences in prayer, simultaneously dealing with my absence at my first child's birth and with all the stresses that come from daily combat operations.

I have been married for about a year and a half, during which time my wife and I lived together in our own home in Germany for only two months before I was deployed. After three months in Baghdad, I was selected to come home on a mid-tour leave for eighteen days, after which I would not see my wife for another year.

We did the math; our biggest fear was that we might conceive while I was home. "O God, please don't let this happen," I prayed. Well, God must have taken that as a challenge instead of a plea, because the morning I got back on the plane for Kuwait, I was looking at a positive pregnancy test my wife had taken.

It took a month or two before it began to really sink in that I was a father. I first felt the weight of our situation when my wife sent me a photo of her belly; she was just starting to show. Suddenly it became real: There was a baby inside of her.

With this realization came bitterness. I kept arguing with God: "All my life I have waited for the day when I could bring my child into this world, and now I am going to miss it? God, how many times did you fill my mind with images in prayer of my wife's pregnant belly with our two hands interlocked around her? This is killing me."

God's response was, "I know." That's it, just "I know"—not exactly the response I was hoping for.

My parents sent me a father-to-be book as a gift, but I soon found myself angry with the author. He talked about how most men don't do this or that for their wives while they are pregnant, like going to the doctor with them. "How does this help me?" I thought. "To hell with those men who don't care, I would do anything to be home right now!"

I found myself trying to make deals with God. I prayed, "God, maybe you could wound me, just badly enough that I can be home to recover in time to be present for the birth."

I tried everything I could to get myself out of my funk. I read numerous books on suffering, two from C.S. Lewis, *The Abolition of Man* and *The Problem of Pain.* All they did was intellectually confirm that it's "OK" for me to suffer.

My prayer then turned to "God, I'll carry this cross, but I am not joyful about it."

To add to my situation, I was running eight-to-twelve-hour night missions on five or six hours of sleep, and my job involved driving down the road looking for bombs that were specifically intended to kill me.

My funk lasted for close to two months; it finally ended on Easter Sunday. I was able to attend Mass after a month of not being able to go, due to missions and the scarcity of Catholic chaplains. I was tired from my mission the night before and wasn't really looking for any solution to what was going on. It was in this sleep-deprived, half-paying-attention state that I had my moment of deep understanding. I finally got it.

For two months all I knew was that I had this huge cross to bear, and I knew that to be an obedient Christian I needed to pick up this cross and continue following Christ. What I didn't understand, what I didn't get before, was where I was walking with this cross—to Calvary. When I told God that it was killing me, I was right, but that was the point all along.

I wasn't going to Calvary alone. The image of carrying my cross came to mind, and I realized that I was looking down, only thinking about the pain and nothing else. For the first time I chose to look up and out. It was then that I realized that this cross will kill me, but if I die with Christ, he promises there will always be a resurrection. I saw that Christ was with me, not to take away my pain but that I might follow him.

The pain and weight of this cross did not go away that Sunday, but what I did find was *hope*. It is that hope that I started taking to my prayer, no longer asking, "God, just end the war in Iraq and send me home." Now each night I thank God for getting me through the day, and I ask him for just one more day.

Step by step I am approaching Calvary, and there are times when I don't think I can make it. But I always seem to make it to the end of the day and to that simple prayer.

A STUDENT

I'll never forget the powerful prayer experience I had at a women's retreat put on by students of Franciscan University of Steubenville. At one point during the retreat, we spent time in adoration before the Blessed Sacrament. I had expected it to go like any other time I had spent in adoration, which usually consisted of my doing most of the "talking." This time was different though.

I decided to try to listen for the Lord's voice. I closed my eyes and sat there for a while, somewhat frustrated that I couldn't hear anything. Then suddenly my mind was at rest, because I could see an image of Jesus. He took my hand and walked with me on a journey through my life—from birth to the present. I didn't know the purpose of the journey until the end of it. I heard him say to me, "Brittany, I have been with you always. I am not far away in the clouds. I am right here with you, living every moment with you." His words brought me so much peace.

After a few moments of silence, I heard him say, "Open your eyes, and look at the women sitting around you. Just as I am fully present with you, I am fully present with them." Though his words were simple and even common sense, it hit me that I hadn't ever fully comprehended his omnipresence, nor had I truly believed in it.

At the end of our time in adoration, I was in tears because of the powerful prayer experience I had just had. Before I got up to leave, I heard the Lord say, "Brittany, I can meet you like this anytime." Since then I have spent more time listening in prayer.

DEEP HEALING

I was training for my first triathlon. This seemed like a big goal, a challenge that could quite possibly be beyond my physical ability but, more than that, take precious time from my family. As I took it to prayer, the issue looked something like this: "Lord, I want so badly to be in your will and have all that I do be for your glory, not mine. If doing this triathlon could glorify you and is in your will, please let me know." My prayer times were filled with peace, day after day.

As for my training, the first time I got out of the pool and into open water, I was terrified. Everything seemed to freeze: I choked on water, and my heart raced like crazy. I kept trying to pray: "Lord, help me, help me. I can't do this alone." I was frustrated and uncertain.

Once again I turned to prayer. "Lord, I want to be in your will; if this triathlon is in your will, please help me know I can do this."

My muscles were freezing, my heart was pounding, and I was praying Hail Marys as fast as I could in hopes that I wouldn't drown. "Lord, I know you have the power to give me peace in this lake. I know I can do this with your help."

As I continued to pray frantically in the lake, I heard, "Shhhh. I'm not asking you to do anything but breathe." I quieted my thoughts and focused on my breathing—in and out, in and out— and just swam.

The next morning I brought this experience to prayer. I quieted my heart, and I asked the Lord where the fear had come from.

A memory from my childhood came to mind. I was with my father near our pool. I fell into the deep end while my father's back was to me. I was drowning, and no one could see. After what seemed like an eternity, my dad finally saw me, jumped in and pulled me from the pool.

As my mind came back to the present, I asked the Lord to continue to reveal to me what he needed me to know about that day in the pool. Once again, quiet peace. My memory was that I almost drowned. The truth was that my father had rescued me. The peace that came was that I do know how to swim, and what I need to remember is to just breathe and trust my Father.

A DEEPER UNDERSTANDING OF WHO I AM

I experienced unjust treatment from someone that left me feeling broken, but praying through the situation led me to a deeper understanding of who God made me to be.

I had always been able to figure things out and fix them before. It was easy to ask the questions: Why did this happen? Why did I receive the consequences of someone else's wounds and insecurities? What could I do to resolve the situation?

It became clear that there was nothing that I could do or say to bring any justice to the situation and make things right again. So I brought *everything* to prayer. I decided to let God reveal and heal. This process took about eight months.

I asked God what he could teach me in the midst of this trial, because I had begun to doubt a lot of the talents he had given me. I also worried about what others thought about me, but I didn't try to defend myself, instead seeking comfort in Jesus' arms. I didn't approach the person who had wronged me and try to change his mind, because I knew that it wouldn't bear any fruit.

I consistently asked God where he was in the situation. I knew that he didn't want this for me but that he could bring good out of it.

A day after my birthday, I was at Mass praying about forgiveness. I knew that I had to forgive this person in my heart, because I was still angry and hurt. Just as I was praying for the grace to forgive, I noticed that this person was also at Mass. I made a very sincere prayer that I was sick of being hurt and angry and that I really wished to forgive him and not have those feelings in my life. I knew that I could never do this on my own.

I received Jesus in the Eucharist and felt a peace that I had not felt in a long time. I knew that God had worked a miracle. God had revealed to me that my worth was not based on anyone except him. He revealed that my gifts did not lose value because someone else did not appreciate them.

Most importantly, God revealed to me that he loved me intimately and shared in my hurt. I was able to offer all of my distress to Jesus on the cross. Jesus was innocent and perfect, and yet he was crucified. I was able to praise God for fathering me so perfectly.

INTIMACY IN PRAYER

When I first heard about the possibility of intimacy in prayer, I felt uncomfortable. At best it seemed appropriate for lonely people who couldn't find enough friends here on earth. I have always been blessed with encouraging and supportive friends and family.

I was spending a good amount of time in prayer every day, yet it took me a long time to recognize my own desire for intimacy. I had no idea why I always "needed" some sort of distraction to fix the ache of my heart. I couldn't sit still in a room unless I had music, television, noise or tobacco. I knew that I felt alone in these moments, but I never realized that only God could dispel this loneliness.

A good friend encouraged me to start praying for intimacy in my relationship with the Lord. Again, something just felt weird about the very word, but the Lord began to open my eyes to see clearly the connection between my ache and the way that he designed me for union with him. It was as if a light was turned on, and I began to see my desire for what it really was. Instead of being overwhelmed by a feeling of loneliness and scrambling to fix it, I was actually grateful to the Lord for using my own feelings and emotions to draw me to himself.

I started taking these prayer times as opportunities to give the Lord my heart. I shared with him what was really on my heart, the good and the bad, in the same way I would share it with another close friend. Of course, he knew the movements of my heart better than I did. But by expressing them, I was beginning to be vulnerable and let the Lord into areas of my life that were previously off-limits to him.

My relationship with the Lord is still a series of his grace and my falls, but learning about intimacy has completely changed the way that I come to him in prayer.

IN SEARCH OF A VOCATION

Several years ago I found myself in a trial of my faith. I had felt called to the priesthood, but after two years in the seminary, I discerned that this was not where God was leading me. In prayer I felt God leading me to go to a particular university, so I applied there, but I was denied.

All I was trying to do was follow God, but everything kept not working out! It seemed as if he had abandoned me. I was living at home, I had no friends and no job, and my only direction had been denied. After several years of trying to follow Christ, I felt that I was at a crossroads. I felt he was asking me to follow when he had seemingly forgotten to show me how.

For several months my only hope came from a daily holy hour. There I prayed, with little response or feeling. My prayer became simply that he would show me the way.

One afternoon the Lord gave me an image during prayer that was transforming. It was an image of me as a child. I was walking hand in hand with God, my Father. We walked to a playground that had been a very prominent place in my childhood. Coming to the edge of the playground, God let go of my hand, looked down at me and said, "Steve, go play." But instead of running away in freedom, I looked back at him and very nervously and anxiously began to question.

"What do you want me to do? Do you want me to swing? Do you want me to go on the playground, or what? Tell me. I don't want to do anything but exactly what you want. What should I do? Tell me."

He just looked at me with confusion. "Stephen," he said and laughed, "go have fun! Follow your heart. Everything is fine with me. No matter what you do, I'll be there for you. Now go play."

I realized that this was the answer to my prayers. God had shown me the way that I was to live. Life was not about making perfect decisions, not about doing everything just right. It was about being loved by God and knowing this. My perspective changed: God loves me, and I need to follow the deep desires he has placed in my heart.

My life is about a relationship with God, and the whole world is the playground. I don't need to figure out everything he desires; I need to love him and let myself be loved by him. The rest he takes care of.

I kept praying, and my prayer was to know his love. Then I went after my heart's desires. Now I am graduating from college, dating a wonderful woman and pursuing a career that I like. At times life still can be really difficult, and I don't always know what he wants me to do. But I do know that he loves me. He has shown me that by spending time with him, what he wants me to do will become clear.

A YOUNG FATHER

My wife and I have been married almost two years. We have a daughter and another one on the way. We moved in with my wife's parents, hoping to save money to buy a home. Now, as we are beginning to look at finally getting a house, we're coming to the realization that we still might not be in a position, financially, to do so.

At first this was a hard realization for me to come to. As "the head of the house," I have always looked at providing for my family as my responsibility. It was hard for me to accept the fact that I was not able to fully do that. My mind was flooded with thoughts and feelings of doubt and inadequacy. I even felt the lie that I was not a good husband and father.

Eventually I took all this to the Lord in prayer. I was really trying to discern where all of this was coming from. As I prayed through it all, Christ reaffirmed my vocation as a husband and father. The feelings of doubt and inadequacy were brought out into the light and revealed as nothing more than lies that the enemy had planted in my heart, trying to discourage me and cause me to doubt my vocation. Jesus showed me that *he*, in fact, would be the one to provide for my family. He wanted me to place my family at his feet in total faith and trust in his plan.

We still don't own our own home, but God has brought me to a place of peace with where our family is right now and especially the role that I am playing in it. I wait on the Lord's plan for our family and on his timing. I know that he has a plan that will bring us hope and joy, that he wants us to live a life of abundance.

I also know that had I not taken all this to prayer and discernment, I might very well be in a very dangerous place of doubt and despair about my vocation.

RESTORATION AND HEALING

My senior year of college was a time of great growth spiritually, emotionally and intellectually. I had spent the summer as an intern in Washington, D.C. I had gone there expecting God to shed some light on my future. Until that point in my life, I had understood God's plan and was generally in agreement with it. I was fairly logical and practical.

Within hours of beginning my internship, I realized that it was going to be very hard to concentrate on anything related to work. I met a young man who was unlike anyone I had ever met before. My heart experienced feelings I had only read about, and suddenly it became difficult to concentrate on anything other than this person. Everything seemed so right. I just knew that God had a plan for me and this person.

But as the summer went on, it became clear to me that this relationship was not going to work out. I left D.C. confused, devastated, unsure, heartbroken yet too prideful and scared to admit it.

I returned to college for my final year, hoping that "out of sight, out of mind" would heal my broken heart. It did little for the pain. I started spiritual direction that fall and found myself explaining that I was unsure of my feelings, of my prayer, of my discernment of God's will in my life.

My greatest fear had been a broken heart. I had tried not to "give my heart away." I had tried to protect myself. I had no idea how I had ended up so broken.

My spiritual director encouraged me to pray about being honest and vulnerable with this young man—something that I had not done. The thought alone challenged me more than anything ever had. Taking it to prayer, Jesus gave me an image of himself hanging on the cross. He gently told me that he endured the cross knowing that he would be rejected by us. He loved freely and totally, knowing that he wouldn't be accepted. His love wasn't dependent on our response. He led me to a quote by C.S. Lewis: "To love at all is to be vulnerable. Love anything, and your heart will certainly be wrung and possibly be broken."[5]

The Lord showed me that in true love there would always be the risk of abandonment, rejection and pain. He endured the risk for us—for the chance of our response to his love.

There was never a moment of complete healing; it was slow and constant. God never abandoned me. In the process he showed me that he allowed my heart to be broken so that it could be rebuilt and restored. It would be much freer and more beautiful when he was done. This was a humbling process, as I had never been compassionate toward anyone struggling with the pain of a hurting heart.

One week after Easter I received an e-mail saying that this young man was engaged. The pain was less than I had expected, but it was real and fresh. I went to pray that evening, and I saw an image of the empty tomb. I saw Mary Magdalene looking for Jesus—devastated, fearful and in mourning. Jesus showed me that she feared the worst. She feared that his body had been taken, when in actuality the most amazing thing had happened.

I was like Mary Magdalene. This news made me fear the worst. Any hope I had held on to for my future seemed crushed. Yet Jesus was inviting me to have hope, for his plans are so much greater than ours. In that moment I experienced the final stages of healing in my heart—a healing that could come only by believing God's promises and trusting in his love.

FINDING IDENTITY

If each of us is created in the image and likeness of God, then our deepest identity is that of his beloved daughter or son. Before we are sisters, brothers, fathers, mothers or friends, we are his children.

After I left the umbrella of college and family, God began to show me how much I placed my worth in other people and in my abilities. I needed affirmation to feel loved, and I would feel shaken if I felt like a failure in any area. In my prayer the Lord began to speak truth into my heart, confirming my identity as his daughter.

I remember one day seeing all of the areas in my life that I thought needed to be "fixed." I was planning how I could work on each area: prayers that I could say, behaviors that I could modify, ways that I could be a better person, friend, daughter and so on. However, in my desire to fix everything for God, I was running from his love. I did not believe that he could accept me in my broken state. I was feeling frustrated and alone.

I finally took a break from trying to figure everything out and cried out in my desperation, "Jesus, what do you want me to do?" The answer in my heart was clear and startling: "Be still, and I will fight for you," he said. "Rest in me. Let me heal you. Let me love you as you are."

In my desire to be pleasing to God and to others, I was trying to fight my battles and protect myself from criticism, disappointment and failure. By shielding myself from those things, I was also shielding myself from receiving authentic love.

Over time I have begun to listen for God's voice. The voice that speaks to me as beloved is often quiet but is always there.

spiritual fecundity and virginal love: a christian anthropology of the heart

Father John Horn, s.j.

> *O that today you would listen to his voice!*
> *Harden not your hearts, as at Meribah.*
>
> (Psalm 95:7–8)

This exhortation by the psalmist presupposes that we know how to listen for and to acknowledge the indwelling voice of the Holy Spirit.

This command in love, this pleading invitation, is rife with a desire for each of us to relate with and receive from the voice of the Holy Spirit alive within our hearts. The psalmist is tasting the truth that God's Spirit leads, guides and passionately loves our souls as no one else can shepherd or love us.

The psalmist knows that we, too, can taste the immediacy of hearing the reality of God's voice—today! Of course, the choice to follow this Chief Shepherd's voice, the voice of the Father's Spirit, is the necessary response that both prevents us from hardening our hearts and gives us hearts that can become abundantly fecund, or fruitful. The interior choosing to respond by following the Holy Spirit as the indwelling Word carries us into an intimate friendship as well as obedient discipleship. It is a way of listening, receiving, choosing and responding—a way of living.

In addition, this interior relating, by which we can permit ourselves to receive love each day, can also carry us into the promise of a self-donating communion, the delight of spousal intimacy and fecundity.

Indeed we know and believe that the Trinity's virginal loving[1] desired to and delighted in creating us out of nothing (*ex nihilo*), that Jesus' Spirit is with us, always desiring and delighting in carrying us into a deeper communion with what is most real and everlasting, the reality of the Father's love and joy.

O that today you would listen to his voice!
Harden not your hearts, as at Meribah.

This living scriptural Word, externally present to us in our hearing, is amazingly pregnant with meaning and new life. In fact, the message and grammar of this small verse foreshadows and helps us understand the pentecostal drama of the Annunciation in Luke 1.

It is in this cataclysmic, history-changing event that Mary acknowledges what is stirring and being spoken in and for her heart. She hears, relates to, receives and humbly responds to the angel's message. Mary's yes as that first disciple maternally mirrors for all of us "the way, the truth and the life" (John 14:6).

Mary's Annunciation foreshadows the ongoing Pentecost that our lives can participate in again and again, as Mary teaches us how to listen, relate to and receive the Holy Spirit's voice in the hiddenness of our Nazareths and our Upper Rooms. Mary's receptivity of the Word magnifies virginal spiritual fecundity in spousal loving. She teaches us that "the most fruitful activity of the human person is to be able to receive God."[2]

The question arises naturally: "How can we listen for, identify, and hearken to God's indwelling voice with wholehearted attention and generosity?"

Saint Paul, as he evangelized the Greeks with his famous speech in the Areopagus, provided us with a vital truth when he said that we "should seek God, in the hope that [we] might feel after him and find him. Yet he is not far from each one of us, for/ 'In him we live and move and have our being.'…'We are indeed his offspring'" (Acts 17:27–28).

In other words, the cards are stacked in our favor. Saint Paul assures us that we can seek God by feeling after him and that, as beloved children, we can readily find him. God is especially near!

So that we might more readily seek him and find him, after providing some operating theological assumptions, I propose to sketch a Christian anthropology of the human heart.[3] I will then apply this way of seeking after, feeling after and finding God to the lives of diocesan priests and seminarians. Hoping that the image of the heart and this outline can help us attend to the Holy Spirit's voice as the indwelling Word, it is important to name briefly seven operating theological assumptions:

▸ God is utterly near (see Isaiah 55:16; John 15:1–11).
▸ God is actively pursuing each of us, desiring a deeper relationship (Hebrews 4:11–13).[4]
▸ Personal subjective experiences that claim to be God's voice are always governed by the objective spiritual authority of Scripture and the Church's living tradition as spoken through the magisterium (Acts 20:17–32).[5]
▸ The Father's Spirit desires only to give consoling love as we live the paschal mystery at the cross with Jesus (2 Corinthians 1:3–7).[6]

▸▸ It is in weakness with Jesus the Christ that we experience the strength of the Holy Spirit (1 Corinthians 1:26–31; 2 Corinthians 12:9–10).

▸▸ True discipleship depends upon a desire to seek after and do the will of God (Luke 1:34–38; Mark 14:32–37).

▸▸ The reign of God is at hand (Matthew 10:5–8; Luke 4:42–43).

With these theological assumptions as a backdrop, I ask you, "How is your heart?" and "Where concretely have you heard God's voice speaking lovingly to you today?" In light of Saint Paul's hope-filled exhortation, I ask you to understand your heart as having three levels of affect or feeling: Level 1: the surface; Level 2: the psychological; Level 3: the spiritual.

Level 1
Surface Feelings, Thoughts, Desires

Level 2
Fundamentally Psychological Feelings, Thoughts, Desires
• Psychological Consolations
• Psychological Desolations

Influenced by:
Family Relationships • Sexual Desires • Ethnic Temperaments • DNA • Deep Moods • Cultural Assumptions
(e.g., money, beauty, customs, myths, ethos, etc.)

Pleasure/Pain Principle

Level 3
Fundamentally Spiritual
• Spiritual Consolations
• Spiritual Desolations
• Affective Movements = Spirits

Intellect   Emotion   Will
(thoughts) (feelings) (choices)

Imagination/Memories

Indwelling Holy Spirit

Our feelings, in the biblical sense of wholeheartedness, are not merely emotions. They connote personhood and a primal affective word (*Urwort*) within that speaks; this is the fundamental meaning of *sentir* in Spanish and *sentire* in Latin.

LEVEL 1: THE SURFACE

To hear God's voice addressing us lovingly, we must not be attentive to Level 1, the surface. Here feelings are very transient and superficial. They change rapidly and are easily swayed by external stimuli, such as the weather and the tone of others' opinions.

The heart's surface movements are also easily affected by the bodily senses' dependence upon the quality and quantity of sleep, food, sunlight and so on. The Holy Spirit's voice as indwelling Word does not subsist and is not heard here.

LEVEL 2: THE PSYCHOLOGICAL

Level 2, the psychological level of affect or feelings, with their accompanying thoughts and desires, are much more complex. Here many factors deeply influence our heart's ongoing affective experience and human development.

These factors include family relationships and ethnic temperaments, which mold and imprint deep patterns of feeling and thinking into the psyche. Our genetic makeup, sexual desires, cultural assumptions regarding beauty and economic security also live here along with deep moods.

All of these factors, factors of nature and nurture, dramatically influence what we are hearing and are carrying in the interior psychological structure or geography of our hearts. Feelings and thoughts, the voices that speak in Level 2, are governed generally by the pleasure/pain principle. According to this psychological principle, we make choices continually to take care of ourselves by making sure that we maintain a healthy balance of tasting the goodness of human pleasure, as we daily live with and endure existential pains. Individuals differ greatly in their distinctive thresholds for pain and the breadth of their comfort zones at this second level.

LEVEL 3: THE SPIRITUAL

It is at Level 3, the spiritual level of our heart's experience, that the indwelling Holy Spirit is readily accessible and can be heard in an everyday living at the cross with Jesus. It is here through baptism that God's voice abides within us[7] and is presently speaking, addressing us with love (John 14:18–31). God's voice is always experienced here as consolation, so long as we are seeking after God so as to do the Father's will.

In a Christian anthropology of the heart, we first want to remember the biblical understanding of the human heart as the deepest place of relation and truth in persons, the seat of spiritual insight and the grounding in faith.[8]

Scripturally, *heart* means "soul." At the center of the human heart is spiritual being. The spiritual realities of the evil one's temptations, which can bind us, and the Holy Spirit's allurements in love are tasted here. Rightly understood, Saint Ignatius Loyola's "Rules for the Discernment of Spirits" are based upon and teach us that the heart's deepest affective movements are spirits.

These affective movements contain the intellect's thoughts, our body's emotions, the will's power to make choices and the creative capacity of imagination.[9] All of these realties or capacities coalesce and run together at the center of our heart's affectivity, at the center of our human spirit.

There are three important biblical truths to remember and to apply at Level 3, as we "feel after" God "and find him" (Acts 17:27):

▸▸ Affective movements are equated with spirits.

▸▸ Spirits include our human spirit, the evil spirit and the Holy Spirit.

▸▸ The Holy Spirit is identifiable with heartfelt consolations in contrast to desolations, so long as the person is seeking after God.[10]

At Level 3 the heart's thoughts, emotions, will and imagination operate within spiritual senses.[11] These spiritual senses can detect, discern and relate, with consolations or desolations, those spiritual movements addressing our souls for ill to bind us or for good to heal us, setting us free for loving service of neighbor.

What matters in prayer, as a heart-to-heart conversation with God, is that we acknowledge and relate anything and everything we are carrying interiorly. This disclosure opens us to receive the Holy Spirit's Word, which actively pursues us to spiritually comfort and to console us, making us one with him (John 14:18–31).

The transforming power of the Holy Spirit's love can be tasted amid everyday activities, if only we would listen for God as indwelling Word while permitting ourselves to receive his love continually:

O that today you would hearken to his voice!
Harden not your hearts as at Meribah.

Needless to say, there are hundreds of synonyms for consolations and desolations that are experienced in our human spirits. Common spiritual desolations include anxiety, loneliness, loss of hope, sadness, boredom, restlessness, fear and discouragement.

Common spiritual consolations include peace, a sense of being loved, hope, joy, zeal, contentment, trustfulness, sadness for sin and courage.

Spiritual desolation points to a dimension of our heart that is lovesick, sick to receive and appropriate more love from God (Matthew 9:12).

Spiritual consolation is a dimension of our being that is conatural with God's Holy Spirit, the Comforter, the Consoler. Spiritual consolation is God's indwelling Word, whenever we are seeking after him, feeling after him so as to find him (see Acts 17:27–28).

> *O that today you would hearken to his voice!*
> *Harden not your hearts as at Meribah.*

We can be predisposed to prayer if we will acknowledge and relate what we are thinking and feeling in our hearts, hoping to hear the Chief Shepherd's voice indwelling. May we seek God, feeling after him so as to find him (Acts 17:27). Pray for each other now, carrying a willingness to receive and respond to the living Word, the Holy Spirit, who is so near! For all of us, may we acknowledge that our primary mission in life is to worship God first.

an operating definition
for christian imagination

Walter J. Burghart, s.j.

First then, what is this creature we call imagination? To begin
with, what is imagination *not*? It is not the same as fantasy.
Fantasy has come to mean the grotesque, the bizarre. The fantas-
tic is unreal, irrational, wild, unrestrained. We speak of "pure fantasy"; it has no connection with reality. It is imagination run wild,
on the loose, unbridled, uncontained.

What is it then? Imagination is the capacity we have "to make
the material an image of the immaterial or spiritual." It is a creative power. You find it in Rembrandt's self-portraits, in
Beethoven's *Fifth Symphony*, in the odor of a new rose or in the
flavor of an old wine. You find it in storytellers like C.S. Lewis and
J.R.R. Tolkien, in dramatists like Aeschylus and Shakespeare, in
poets from Sappho to e.e. cummings.

Now when I say "capacity," I do not mean a "faculty" like
intellect or will. I mean rather a posture of our whole person
toward our experiences. It is a way of seeing. It is as with
Castaneda, looking for holes in the world or listening to the space
between sounds. It is a breaking through the obvious, the surface,
the superficial, to the reality beneath and beyond. It is the world
of wonder and intuition, of amazement and delight, of festivity
and play.[1]

APPENDIX THREE
prayer: a personal response to God's presence

Father Armand M. Nigro, s.j.

I am convinced that at the basis of all that we term a crisis is a crisis of faith. But there is no hope for improvement here unless individual persons begin to respond better to God in prayer. Either we are not praying correctly or we have stopped praying. This is true, I think, both of laypeople and of us religious.

The single, most important conviction I want to share with you is that *prayer is a personal response to God's presence*. May I try to explain this?

Either you and I are more important than God or God is more important than we are. The answer is obvious, isn't it? He is more important than we are. Further, if what God wants and does is more important than what we want or do, then more of our attention should be focused on what God is and does. Again, what God wants to say to us is more important for us than anything we may have to say to him. And God does want to speak and communicate himself to us.

When prayer becomes too self-centered, even if it is centered upon noble and holy desires, if the focus of our prayer is I, me or my, we are going to be in difficulty.

Prayer is a personal response to God's presence. This means that God first makes himself present to us. Prayer is our awareness and acknowledgement of God's presence. It is what God does to us, rather than anything we do. Saint John reminds us that genuine love means first of all not that we love God (which may or may not be true) but that God first loves us. His love for us is more important than our love for him. He wants and appreciates and is grateful for our love; but since his love for us is more important than our love for him, his love deserves more of our attention.

It seems to me that there are three aspects of genuine prayer that we should keep in mind. First of all, if prayer is a personal response to God's presence, then the beginning of prayer is to be *aware* of that presence, simply to acknowledge it, to be able to admit: "Yes, God my Father, you do love life into me. Yes, you love life and being into the things around me and into all that comes into my senses. You love talents and these longings into me, etc." The focus is on God and what God does.

I want to make a distinction. I know that the terms *meditation* and *prayer* are used interchangeably and that they are used differently by different authors. By "religious meditation" I mean thinking about God or what God does or about anything good, holy or pious; but this is not prayer. When I am thinking about you, you are the focal point of my thoughts, but that is not *communication with* you. Prayer is a person-to-person communication with God. If I am thinking about God or the life of Christ and what he has done, that is holy, meritorious, good and helpful for prayer; but it is not essentially prayer.

Prayer is when "he" becomes "you," when I say, "Yes, God my Father, you love life into me." When I say to myself, "God loves life into me," that is a meditation. Do you see how I am using the words? When there is a you-I relationship with the Father, Son and Spirit, I call this response genuine prayer. If there is a consideration of what he is and does, but not a you-I relationship, it may be helpful, good and holy, but it is not essentially prayer.

The basis or first step in prayer is for me to wake up and face reality; to realize that he is present to me, that he loves breathing a share of his own divine life and all my capacities into me, and to be able to say, "Yes, God my Father, you do love all this into me. Yes, Jesus my brother, you do. Yes, God my Spirit, you do." That is to pray. If in the few minutes that we have during the times of private prayer, we do nothing else but merely make ourselves aware of the God who is already making himself present to us, that experience in itself is profound prayer; it is fruitful prayer; it is even the beginning of mystical prayer. This is a genuine opening up to God, who communicates himself to us if we only give him the opportunity.

There is a difference between persons and things. God is present to things; God saturates things with his presence, because he loves life and being into them. But there is no acknowledgment on the part of non-personal things; they are incapable of prayer. You and I, however, because we are persons, can acknowledge that presence; and that is the first step in prayer.

The second step, it seems to me, is that once we realize what God is to us, what he does for us and how much he loves us, the only decent, polite, obvious and spontaneous response is not only to say, "Yes, you do," but also "Thank you, God my Father, for loving life, being and a share of your own nature into me. Thank you, Jesus, God the Son and my brother. Thank you, God the Holy Spirit, for living on in me." Gratitude is an obvious, spontaneous outflow of being aware of what God is and is doing for us.

As an analogy, if a person is very good to me and unselfish and financially supports me, but I do not know him or realize this, I cannot respond to his goodness and love. But if I find out that my support is coming from him, that many good things that make my life much better are coming from him, personally, uniquely to me, it's one thing when I begin to realize and acknowledge it: "Yes, he does. Yes, you do." And something more when I say: "Thank you."

Do you notice the focus of this response? It is essential for gratitude that there be an awareness of receiving from another. No one opens a door into a strange and dark room, where he sees nothing, and begins to converse into the room just in case there might be somebody there. Rather we are first conscious of someone; we look into someone's eyes; we are assured that if we talk into this microphone, there is a radio audience waiting on our words; or if we look into that camera, there is a TV audience present; or if we put our words on tape, somebody will listen to them. We speak and respond only to some kind of personal presence.

Prayer is like that. Sometimes in our good and holy desires to communicate with God, we "junk-up" our prayer. We begin immediately to make acts of faith, hope or love, of contrition or sorrow; we ask for things or just say something, because, after all, we can't just sit there and let nothing happen; so we do something, *we* say something! I call this "junking-up" our prayer. If we do that before we are really conscious of God being present to us, it is like opening up a dark room and talking because there might be somebody there who might possibly be listening. It is important that we take time peacefully and quietly (even if we have only a few minutes to pray) *first* to make ourselves aware of the loving, creative, sustaining, divinizing presence of God, because prayer is a personal response to God's presence.

The first step, then, is to acknowledge God's presence; the second is to thank him. *The third* is a loving response. A person responds to love freely given by saying, "I love you, *too*." When we say this to God, it implies that we first become aware that he first loves us. To say, "God my Father, Christ my brother, God my Holy Spirit, I love you too," is our response at its best.

With regard to asking God for favors, I hope we don't misunderstand it as imperfect prayer. When we beg God for sunny weather, or pray that our bursitis will go away, or pray for something more holy or important such as international peace and justice, we pay a great compliment to God. This is an expression of "becoming as little children," which Jesus recommended and honored. A child who comes to his parents and asks for things is paying them a big compliment. What is the child saying but "You are good and can fill my needs. Please, may I have a candy bar?"

When we approach God with this sense of our absolute, total dependence and need, we are conscious of being precious and important, but without him of being nothing, because all that we have is loved into us by God. In this consciousness we are profoundly acknowledging what he is and what we are. Did not Jesus himself say: "When you pray, face God and say *Abba* [Hebrew baby talk for "Papa" or "Daddy"], give us this day our daily bread, forgive us our offences, lead us not into temptation, deliver us from evil"? Notice how much of the Our Father is petition. Our Lord teaches us to pray this way. If the prayer of petition is made correctly, it says, "God, you are everything; Creator, Sustainer, Divinizer, Forgiver, Merciful Lord of the Universe, Provident God of all, I belong completely to you." When we pray for any favor, we mean, of course, "Thy will be done." We are not trying to blackmail or fool God into giving us something by groveling in his presence. No, we presuppose, "Thy will be done"—but we still would like to have a sunny day tomorrow, etc.

To return to an earlier point: What God does is more important than what we do. And God longs to communicate himself to us. The tragedy is that so few of us permit God to communicate himself to us in prayer. One reason for this failure is faulty teaching or education in prayer. A second is a lack of trust or faith that he really wants to and is going to communicate himself personally and uniquely to us. Since we feel uncertain about this, we do most or all of the talking or meditating, or we fill the time with spiritual reading or something "profitable," but we are reluctant to empty ourselves and abandon ourselves to his presence and movement so that in silence he can communicate himself to us the way he prefers.

A third reason is that we are afraid of failing, afraid of trying this kind of prayer and finding out that it doesn't work for us. It will always work, if we remove obstacles and give God a chance, because God longs to communicate himself to each of us personally. He wants to make our prayer more and more mystical. And this is not in any dangerous, quietist, way-out, extraordinary sense. God wants us to be normal, ordinary, everyday healthy mystics. By mystic I mean the sort of person who opens up to God's presence, who lets God fill his consciousness with his personal presence. The older we grow in our prayer life, the more aware, sensitive, attuned, docile, responsive to God's presence we become; because all genuine prayer is a personal response to that presence.

We have developed or been given two different kinds of capacities or facilities with which to respond or act socially or otherwise. One set of habits we call virtues. These are active capacities; they enable us to do things, and through our activity we perfect these habits. They are acquired by activity; sometimes the beginnings of them are infused, but at least they can be perfected and made stronger by exercise, and they render our virtuous activity easier. They are the "can do" of our operating capacities and are very important. But there are also capacities loved into us by God which enable us to be receptive. A radio station not only has a transmitter, but it also has a receiver; they are both important. These receptive capacities become more and more important in our prayer life. They are called gifts of the Holy Spirit. They make us aware, and receptive, attuned, sensitive, responsive, docile to

God's communicating presence; and he wants us to pray more and more that way.

All growth in prayer, then, is rooted in our conviction that God is present to us, that his presence is personal, loving and provident, uniquely saturating us; that God is and wants more and more to be our Father, and that like every good father, God wants to speak and communicate with us. He keeps trying to speak to us through all the experiences of our life, through his Church, through his living work in Holy Scripture, through his eternal Word Jesus Christ, in whose Holy Spirit we are invited to be sons and daughters. God, I repeat, longs to communicate himself to us, and he invites us to listen and receive. But he will not force this on us.

Now, may I make some practical suggestions? I said that some of us are afraid to give God a chance, because we fear it may not work. But it will work (that's a guarantee) if we give him a chance. In practice, what can we do in order to enable God to communicate himself more fully and freely to us?

Try to be faithful to at least fifteen to thirty minutes of daily being alone with God. Try to make room for this at a regular time each day. God wants time to be alone with each of us and communicate with us; and what God wants from us God deserves. Can you remember five *P*s of prayer?

1. *Passage* from Holy Scripture (choose one). Before beginning your prayer period, choose a short passage of five to ten verses from the Bible. This is very important. Never omit this before your prayer period, either the evening before or the first few minutes before you begin to pray. Choose a passage that you want especially to listen to, to taste and savor and relish. It may be a favorite psalm or parable or miracle story or section of one of Our Lord's sermons. It should fit your mood and your need. Put a

marker in the page and keep it ready. You may or may not come back to it before your prayer period ends.

2. *Place.* Find a private spot where you can be alone with God. This is important. Sometimes it is good to be in the presence of the Blessed Sacrament, but if people are in the chapel with you and you feel like stretching out your arms, if you feel like throwing back your head or looking up, if you feel like sighing or complaining or crying or dancing or singing, you will not do it. But you can do this when you are alone; you should feel free to do this. Otherwise you are inhibiting yourself. You must not be inhibited when you respond to God's presence. So pick a quiet place where you are alone and can uninhibitedly speak and react to God's presence without drawing attention from others.

3. *Posture.* At the beginning of private prayer, take the time to settle yourself peacefully. You do not pray as an angel or disembodied spirit or as an intellect: but you pray as a man or a woman. Men and women have bodies, and bodily posture is important in prayer. Do you pray better when kneeling? Then kneel. Do you feel more receptive and open to God's presence when sitting? Then sit. Our founder, Saint Ignatius, was a mystic who seemed to prefer lying down during his prayer and recommends that we try it, too.

Experiment with various postures till you find one most conducive for responding to God's presence. This may vary from day to day and within the same prayer period. Try, for example, lying on the bed or sitting in a comfortable chair with your feet propped on a stool and arms resting on arm rests or on your lap with palms up; or sitting in a hard-backed chair with palms facing up or down on your lap, with head back and jaw relaxed; or standing (perhaps leaning against something) with head comfortably back; or sitting at a table or desk with arms resting on it; or kneeling with arms resting on a support or outstretched, etc., etc. Different postures fit our different moods and needs.

4. *Presence* of God. Respond to God's presence. Peacefully remind yourself how present he is to you. Feel, for example, the cloth of your clothes or the desk in front of you, and admit to God, "Yes, you love feeling into me and texture into it. You love sight into me and color into it. You love hearing into me and sound into it. You love life into me. You are in me. Thank you for living in me, for loving goodness and sonship or daughterhood into me." This takes a little time, but it should always be done and never rushed. You should not hurry that part of your prayer, even if it takes up the whole time. You may feel like saying, "Thank you. I love you, too." In these moments God's special communication may come with that deep personal sense of his presence. Sometimes he makes his presence felt (experienced) by us. And when he does, let it continue; let this experience hold or carry you, just as water holds up a floating body. Stay with it until it fades. Do not move away from it or change or rush the experience or overreact with too many or unnecessary words. We tend to "junk up" our prayer with too many words. Perhaps a simple repetition of "My Lord and my God" or "Abba, Father" will do. If it fades, continue the reminders that you have of his presence.

5. *Passage* from Scripture (return to it and listen to it). There may be no time left to read the Scripture passage you selected. If so, fine. But when you try to respond to God's

presence in a grateful, loving and adoring way, if nothing seems to happen, if you feel dry and desolate, do not be discouraged or judge this as a sign of failure. Rather, the dryness may be God inviting you to listen to him as he speaks to you in Holy Scripture. Always have the Scriptures available when you are at prayer; never be without them. When nothing seems to happen after trying patiently and peacefully to respond to God's presence, when you feel he is not communicating himself, turn to the place you selected in Scripture and give him a chance to communicate himself to you. Listen while he talks, because Scripture is the living Word of the living God; it is living now because God is alive now, and he hasn't changed his mind in what he said through the inspired writers. It is more important to listen this way to God than to speak.

Very slowly with attention whisper or read aloud (not silently) God's words. Pause between the phrases so that the echo and meaning of the words can sink into you slowly, like soft rain into thirsty soil. You may want to keep repeating a word or phrase. If you finish the selected passage, go back and slowly repeat it (just as we repeat the chorus of a song).

Why whisper or speak aloud the words of Scripture? Because this engages our attention more fully through eyes, ears and voice. Often when I read something in silence, my eyes focus on the words while my imagination and attention wander far away.

Praying with Scripture this way is an experience of listening to God. Do not try to make applications or search for profound meanings or implications or conclusions or resolutions. These usually "junk up" our prayer.

> Be content to listen simply and openly as a child who climbs into its papa's lap and listens to a story.

When the time is up, thank God for speaking to you. Realize that Father, Son and Spirit live on in you as you move away to continue the rest of your day.

These are my suggestions for permitting God to communicate himself to us. Even if we have lived long years of half-distracted, half-tepid, halfhearted attempts at praying, it is never too late—even if we are 107 years old. Try it. Taste and see for yourself. I promise that within a very short time, God will make a real mystic out of you if you give him this opportunity and remain faithful to it. By mystic I mean a very normal, healthy, ordinary, everyday sort of mystic graced with the kind of prayer that God longs to communicate to us.

Perhaps I should clarify the word *mystic*. By *mystic* I mean any conscious union of God with humans, initiated and sustained by God; it is an experience which we cannot make, earn or be responsible for. You cannot initiate or sustain it yourself. Sometimes even when we do not put very much effort into prayer, God seems very present. He fills us with his consolation. It's a wonderful experience. We feel loving and more loved ourselves. And the next day we may put in more effort than before, but nothing happens; ashes seem to fill our heart; there is no taste for prayer, even though we hunger for it. God seems a thousand miles away. It may not be that we do anything wrong. Rather, God is teaching us. He is teaching us that we cannot make, earn, deserve or force this sort of experience. It is freely given: a mystical experience.

There are many words to describe this experience: consolation, peace, joy and a feeling of greater faith and hope, of being loved, of being more loving. It is initiated by God. He is anxious to communicate in this way. Then why doesn't he do it more often, if he is so anxious? One reason is, God cannot abide with or reward error or falsehood. Before he can console and communicate himself to us, we have to remove obstacles and make it possible for him to come into our lives. He will not force his friendship on us. One of the prerequisites is that we be convinced, not merely intellectually but deep down in our inner selves, that this is something we cannot make, steal, earn, deserve. This is totally and freely given. We can only dispose ourselves to receive it. We can prepare ourselves for it and be deeply grateful when it comes. When it comes we can humbly say, "Why me? I don't deserve this; but I am grateful for it." That is mystical experience. And it is not always as ecstatic as it might sound; most often it is very quiet, peaceful, a simple inward assurance that God is with me and I am loved by him. It is really not very definable at all.

Mysticism *par excellence* is the Incarnation, that union of the human and divine, initiated by the Divine, in Jesus the Man-God. All other mysticism is but a participation more or less in the reality of the Incarnation. It is a sharing in it, and that is what God wants. He became a man in order to share his divinity with us.

The kind of person God wants you to be, the kind of grace and prayer he is offering to you and desires so much to give you, is to enable you to be a profoundly prayerful person, a genuine contemplative all day long, no less in manual work or in suffering than during the Divine Office or at the sacrifice of the Mass. Private prayer is essential to this. My effort in private prayer does not earn the grace; that is, if I set aside time for it, that isn't going to guarantee it automatically. We don't put in a nickel's worth of human effort and get back a nickel's worth of mystical experience. But we should faithfully give time every day to private prayer, and this in turn enables us to find God in all other things. It makes our liturgical and community prayer better. It makes our work and social involvements more of an experience with God. Our work, in turn, which is an experience with God, feeds our desire for prayerful union with God and enables us to pray better when we do have ten or fifteen minutes or half an hour of private prayer to spend with him alone. The two feed on and nourish each other.

All of us can be prayerful in this way. God wants us to be and is longing to make us prayerful. If we respond to him, each of us will become prayerful in a very unique way. Each of us is unique; our response is unique: God's love and presence is also unique.

a suggestion for family or group prayer

1. After dinner, before dishes are cleared away (or any preferable time), select a short passage from the Bible, for example, Mark 4:35–40. Usually Dad is reader; others can be.

2. Dad first invites those present to listen carefully to God's Word and reminds them of Jesus' assurance: "Where two or three are gathered in my name, I am there, too." He begins with a short prayer, such as "Speak to us, Lord. Help us listen carefully to your word."

3. Then he reads the passage aloud very slowly, distinctly, with pauses, so that each phrase can sink into the listeners.

4. After the reading, each in turn shares what it said to him personally: "I felt this..." "I heard this..." "This struck me..." "To me it said or meant..." Keep contributions very short, personal (say "I" not "we"), honest, simple, not preachy, not applying lessons to others. Be careful not to make this a discussion. That will kill the prayer experience. Peacefully, humbly, sensitively listen to God's Word, and simply share what it said and meant to you personally.

    Do not feel uneasy during silent gaps between readings or comments. These silent moments are golden and afford rare opportunities of letting God's message resonate and slowly deepen in us. Relax. Savor his words during the silences.

5. After the first round of sharing, Dad again reads the same passage slowly. It is a richer listening experience this time, because the remarks each one shared have enriched the passage for the others. God speaks to all through each other too.

6. A second round of sharing, usually richer than the first, follows the second reading.

7. The same passage is read slowly a third and last time.

8. After the third reading, only spontaneous prayers are spoken directly to God the Father or to Jesus or to the Holy Spirit or to our Blessed Mother—for example, "Thank you, Jesus, for speaking to us. Help me be more aware of your presence in me and in others."

9. After each has spontaneously prayed, a favorite hymn can be sung, and the clean-up in the kitchen begins (or whatever else follows).

It is hard to limit this to a half hour, because minutes fly by.

God's presence becomes very real, especially during the prayers. While one prays aloud, the others are not mere listeners but join in spirit and make that prayer their own.

This group sharing and praying with Scripture is excellent for other groups—clubs, classrooms, Sodality and C.C.D., married couples' groups, ecumenical or other Christian settings. It works best with ten people or less. When more are present, it may be wise to break into smaller groups. Discuss it afterward to improve it.

We call this a *collatio* [pronounced *coh-LAH-tsee-oh*], a Latin word for "a shared meal," to which everyone contributes and in which we all share.

Try it. Treat your family or group to a real prayer experience. I've seen the *collatio* transform the religious life of families and groups, even of religious communities.

APPENDIX **FIVE**
praying with scripture

Father Armand M. Nigro, s.j. and
Father John F. Christensen, s.j.

GOD SPEAKS TO US FIRST

This fundamental truth makes it possible for us to pray to God. He
has been concerned for each of us long before we became concerned for ourselves.

He desires communication with us.

He speaks to us continually, revealing himself to us by various modes:

▸▸ through Jesus Christ, his Word;

▸▸ through the Church, the extension of Christ in the world
(because we are joined together in Christ, God speaks to
us through other people);

▸▸ through visible creation around us, which forms the
physical context of our lives (Creation took place in his
Son, and it is another form of God's self-revelation);

▸▸ through the events of our lives;

▸▸ through Holy Scripture, a real form of his presence. This
is the mode of communication we are most concerned
with in prayer.

HE INVITES US TO LISTEN

Our response to God's initial move is to listen to what he is saying. This is the basic attitude of prayer.

What you do immediately before prayer is very important. Normally prayer is something you do not rush right into. Spend a few minutes quieting yourself and relaxing, settling yourself into a prayerful and comfortable position.

In listening to anyone, you try to tune out everything except what the person is saying to you.

In prayer this can be done best in *silence* and *solitude.* Select a favorite passage from Holy Scripture, five to ten verses. Put a marker in the page. Try to find a quiet place where you can be alone and uninhibited in your response to God's presence. Try to quiet yourself interiorly. Jesus would often go up a mountain by himself to pray with his Father.

In an age of noise, activity and tensions like our own, it is not always easy or necessary to forget our cares and commitments, the noise and excitement of our environment. Never feel constrained to blot out all distractions. Anxiety in this regard could get between ourselves and God.

Rather, realize that the Word did become flesh—that he speaks to us in the noise and confusion of our day. Sometimes in preparing for prayer, relax and listen to the sounds around you. God's presence is as real as they are.

Be conscious of your sensations and living experiences of feeling, thinking, hoping, loving, of wondering, desiring and so on. Then, conscious of God's unselfish, loving presence in you, address him simply and admit: "Yes, you do love life and feeling into me. You do love a share of your personal life into me. You are present to me. You live in me. Yes, you do."

God is present *as a person*, in you through his Spirit, who speaks to you now in Scripture, and who prays in you and for you.

Ask God for the grace to listen to what he says.

Begin reading Scripture slowly and attentively. Do not hurry to cover much material.

If it recounts an event of Christ's life, be there in the mystery of it. Share with the persons involved, for example, a blind man being cured. Share their attitude. Respond to what Jesus is saying.

Some words or phrases carry special meaning for you. Savor those words, turning them over in your heart.

You may want to speak or recite a psalm or other prayer from Scripture. Really mean what you are saying.

When something strikes you, for example:

▸▸ you feel a new way of being with Christ. He becomes *for you* in a new way (for example, you sense what it means to be healed by Christ),

▸▸ you experience God's love,

▸▸ you feel lifted in spirit,

▸▸ you are moved to do something good,

▸▸ you are peaceful,

▸▸ you are happy and content just to be in God's presence,

this is the time to *pause.*

This is God speaking directly to you in the words of Scripture. Do not hurry to move on. Wait until you are no longer moved by the experience.

Don't get discouraged if nothing seems to be happening.

Sometimes God lets us feel dry and empty in order to let us realize it is not in our own power to communicate with him or to experience consolation. God is sometimes very close to us in his seeming absence (Psalm 139:7–8). He is for us entirely in a self-less way. He accepts us as we are, with all our limitations—even with our seeming inability to pray. A humble attitude of listening is a sign of love for him and a real prayer from the heart.

At these times remember the words of Paul: "The Spirit, too comes to help us in our weakness, for when we cannot choose words in order to pray properly, the Spirit himself expresses our plea in a way that could never be put into words" (Romans 8:26–27).

Relax in prayer. Remember, God will speak to you in his own way. "Yes, as the rain and snow come down from the heavens and do not return without watering the earth, making it yield and giving growth to provide seed for the sower and bread for the eating, so the word that goes from my mouth does not return to me empty, without carrying out my will and succeeding in what it was sent to do" (Isaiah 55:10–11).

Spend time in your prayer just being conscious of God's presence in and around you. If you want to, speak with him about the things you are interested in or wish to thank him for, your joys, sorrows, aspirations and so on.

SUMMARY: FIVE Ps

1. *Passage* from Scripture. Pick one and have it marked and ready.
2. *Place.* Where you are alone and uninhibited in your response to God's presence.
3. *Posture.* Relaxed and peaceful. A harmony of body with spirit.
4. *Presence of God.* Be aware of it and acknowledge and respond to it. If nothing happens turn to the
5. *Passage* from Scripture. Read it very slowly aloud, and listen carefully and peacefully to it.

Read aloud or whisper in a rhythm with your breathing—a phrase at a time—with pauses and repetitions when and where you feel like it.

Don't be anxious; don't try to look for implications or lessons or profound thoughts or conclusions or resolutions and so on. Be content to be like a child who climbs into the father's lap and listens to his words and his story. When you finish, remind yourself that God continues to live in you during the rest of the day.

INTRODUCTION: another book on prayer?

1. Ernest W. Nicholson, *The Book of the Prophet Jeremiah, Chapters 26–52* (New York: Cambridge University Press, 1975), p. 71.

2. Augustine, *Confessions*, Henry Chadwick, trans. (New York: Oxford University Press, 1998), p. 3.

CHAPTER ONE: why prayer is important

1. Mother Teresa, *No Greater Love*, Becky Benenate and Joseph Durepos, eds. (Novato, Calif.: New World Library, 2002), p. 3.

2. Jacques Philippe, *Time for God: A Guide to Prayer* (Boston: Pauline, 1992), p. 28.

3. Mother Teresa, *No Greater Love*, pp. 7–8.

4. William K. Kilpatrick, *Why Johnny Can't Tell Right From Wrong* (New York: Touchstone, 1993), p. 196.

5. Ignatius of Loyola, Rule 12 of Rules for Discernment, in Timothy M. Gallagher, O.M.V. *The Discernment of Spirits: An Ignatian Guide for Everyday Living* (New York: Crossroad, 2005), p. 151.

6. John of the Cross, *Obras Completas* as translated in Philippe, pp. 31–32.

7. Jean-Baptiste Chautard, *The Soul of the Apostolate* (Trappist, Ky.: Abbey of Gethsemani, 1946), pp. 52–53, quoting Saint Bernard, Sermon 18 in *Cantica*.

8. Teresa of Avila, *The Life of Teresa of Jesus,* E. Allison Peers, trans. (New York: Image, 1960), p. 183.

CHAPTER TWO: cultural realities

1. *New American Bible* (Washington: United States Conference of Catholic Bishops, 2002), Exodus 1:8 footnote.

2. Frederich Nietzsche, *The Gay Science* (New York: Vintage, 1974), p. 181.

3. Richard Dawkins, *The God Delusion* (New York: Houghton Mifflin, 2008), p. 51.

4. Branden Hayes Henline, doctoral dissertation, *Technology use and intimacy development in committed relationships: exploring the*

influence of differentiation of self, Texas Digital Library,
http://repositories.tdl.org.

5. Pope Benedict XVI, January 8, 2006, Homily, available at:
    www.vatican.va.

6. Walt Mueller, "10 surprising things you need to know about today's
    youth culture," available at: www.pastors.com.

7. Pope John Paul II, *Redemptoris Hominis*, 10, available at: www.
    vatican.va.

8. Walt Mueller, "Brokenness ... deep and wide," The Center for
    Parent/Youth Understanding, 2006, www.cpyu.org. 2004 statistics
    are from "Marriage and Divorce," *National Center for Health
    Statistics,* February 28, 2006, available at: www.cdc.gov; quote is
    from "The State of Our Unions: The Social Health of Marriage in
    America" (Piscataway, N.J.: The National Marriage Project, 2005), p.
    18; final statement is from www.divorcereform.org.

9. Alan Guttmacher Institute, available at: www.abortiontv.com.

10. Joseph Ratzinger, *Without Roots: The West, Relativism, Christianity,
    Islam* (New York: Basic, 2006), p. 128.

CHAPTER THREE: straight to the heart

1. James Hastings, ed., *A Dictionary of the Bible* (New York: Charles
    Scribner's Sons, 1910), vol. 2, p. 317.

2. John M'Clintock and James Strong, eds., *Cyclopedia of Biblical,
    Theological, and Ecclesiastical Literature* (Grand Rapids: Baker,
    1969), vol. 4, p. 114.

3. M'Clintock and Strong, p. 114.

4. "Levels of the Heart" is a unique term provided by the Institute for
    Priestly Formation. For further development of this term and the
    broader "Christian Anthropology of the Heart," see Appendix One,
    "Spiritual Fecundity and Virginal Love, A Christian Anthropology
    of the Heart," by Father John Horn, S.J.

5. Simon Tugwell, *Prayer: Living with God* (Springfield, Ill.:
    Templegate, 1975), pp. 11–12.

6. Mother Teresa, *Come Be My Light: The Private Writings of the "Saint of Calcutta,"* Brian Kolodiejchuk, ed. (New York: Doubleday, 2007), p. 187.

7. Richard Umbers, "Mother Teresa's agony," available at: www.mercatornet.com.

8. Gallagher, *The Discernment of Spirits*, pp. 114–115, emphasis mine.

CHAPTER FOUR: know your enemy

1. Frank Sheed, *Theology and Sanity* (San Francisco: Ignatius, 1978), p. 188.

2. Gallagher, *The Discernment of Spirits*, quoting Ignatius' twelfth rule, p. 151.

3. See Gallagher, *The Discernment of Spirits*, p. 7.

4. Gallagher, *The Discernment of Spirits*, p. 31.

CHAPTER FIVE: prayer principles

1. Francis de Sales, *Introduction to the Devout Life*, John K. Ryan, trans. (New York: Image, 1989), p. 88.

CHAPTER SEVEN: imagine that!

1. See Appendix Two for an operating definition of Christian imagination.

2. Francis de Sales, p. 85.

3. Sheed, p. 31.

CHAPTER EIGHT: make it a habit

1. Gallagher, *The Discernment of Spirits*, p. 31.

2. Francis de Sales, p. 81.

3. Francis de Sales, pp. 84–86.

4. Francis de Sales, p. 86.

5. Francis de Sales, p. 86.

6. Francis de Sales, p. 87.

7. Francis de Sales, pp. 87–89.

8. Francis de Sales, p. 89.

9. Timothy M. Gallagher, O.M.V. *The Examen Prayer: Ignatian Wisdom for Our Lives Today* (New York: Crossroad, 2006), pp. 20–21.

10. Adapted from Gallagher, *The Examen Prayer* and from Father Scott Traynor, Learning the Love of God Seminar, session 2 handout, "The Consciousness Examen."

11. Pope Benedict XVI, Message to the Youth of the World on the Occasion of the Twenty-first World Youth Day, Palm Sunday, April 9, 2006, available at: www.vatican.va.

12. Pope Benedict XVI, Address to the International Congress Commemorating the Fortieth Anniversary of *Dei Verbum*, September 16, 2005, available at: www.vatican.va.

13. Adapted from Armand M. Nigro, "Prayer: A Personal Response to God's Presence." For full text of article, see Appendix Three.

CHAPTER NINE: the journey

1. Leo the Great, Sermon 22, 3, *Patrologia Latina* 54, 192C, in *Office of Readings*, Friday of the fifth week of ordinary time.

2. Sheed, p. 361.

3. Sheed, pp. 26–27.

4. Sheed, p. 27.

5. Sheed, p. 298.

6. Sheed, pp. 445, 454–455.

7. Sheed, p. 455.

8. Sheed, p. 455.

9. Sheed, p. 458.

10. Pedro Arrupe spoke these words to a group of religious sisters. Quoted by Kevin F. Burke, "Pedro Arrupe's Mysticism of Open Eyes," Jesuit School of Theology at Berkeley, available at: www.jstb.edu.

11. Sheed, p. 344.

12. Ralph Martin, *The Fulfillment of All Desire: A Guidebook for the Journey to God Based on the Wisdom of the Saints* (Steubenville, Ohio: Emmaus Road, 2006), p. 443.

CHAPTER TEN: testimonies

1. Bernard of Clairvaux, *On the Song of Songs*, Kilian Walsh, trans. (Kalamazoo, Mich.: Cistercian, 1976), vol. 2, p. 188.

2. Bernard of Clairvaux, vol. 1, p. 19.

3. Thérèse of Lisieux, *Story of a Soul*, John Clarke, O.C.D., trans. (Washington, D.C.: ICS, 1972), p. 200.

4. John of the Cross, *The Spiritual Canticle*, stanza 39, no. 7, in Kieran Kavanaugh and Otilio Rodriguez, trans., *The Collected Works of Saint John of the Cross*, rev. ed. (Washington, D.C.: ICS, 1991), p. 624.

5. C.S. Lewis, *The Four Loves* (New York: Harcourt, 1960), p. 121.

APPENDIX ONE: spiritual fecundity and virginal love: a christian anthropology of the heart

1. See Gregory Nazianzus, *Poems I*, 2, cited by Raniero Cantalamessa, *Virginity*, p. 16.

2. J. Corbon, *The Wellspring of Worship*, p. 21.

3. X. Leon-Dufour, *Dictionary of the New Testament*, p. 222.

4. See also, for example, Augustine, *Confessions*, C.S. Lewis, *Surprised by Joy*, Thérèse of Lisieux, *Story of a Soul*.

5. See also *Lumen Gentium*, 22.

6. This is the spiritual theology that animates Saint Ignatius Loyola's "Rules for the Discernment of Spirits."

7. Gregory of Nyssa, *On the Beatitudes*, 6; see *The Liturgy of the Hours*, vol. 3, p. 413.

8. J. Horn, *Mystical Healing*, p. 1.

9. W. Burghardt, *Sir, We Would Like to See Jesus*, p. 5. See also Appendix Two.

10. H. Egan, *The Ignatian Mystical Horizon*, pp. 75–77.

11. Diadochus of Photice, *Treatise on Spiritual Perfection*, 6; see *The Liturgy of the Hours* vol. 3, pp. 154–155.

APPENDIX TWO: an operating definition for christian imagination

1. Burghardt, *Sir, We Would Like to See Jesus* (New York: Paulist, 1982), p. 5.